Grandmothers

Grandmothers

by Lauren Cowen and Jayne Wexler

stewart tabori & chang

Published in 2005 by
Stewart, Tabori & Chang
115 West 18th Street
New York, NY 10011
www.abramsbooks.com

Canadian Distribution:
Canadian Manda Group
165 Dufferin Street
Toronto, Ontario M6K 3H6
Canada

Library of Congress Cataloging-in-Publication Data
Cowen, Lauren.
Grandmothers / by Lauren Cowen and Jayne Wexler.
p. cm.
ISBN 1-58479-465-8
1. Grandmothers—United States. 2. Grandparent and child—United States. 3. Grandchildren—United States. I. Wexler, Jayne. II. Title.

HQ759.9.C67 2005
306.874'5'0973—dc22
2005007670
Designed by Maria Taffera Lewis/Blue Studio Design.

The text of this book was composed in Garamond and Bickham Script.

Printed in Singapore

10 9 8 7 6 5 4 3 2 1

First Printing

LA MARTINIÈRE
GROUPE

In memory of my parents, Judy and Howard Silverman,
whose love for their grandchildren will last for generations.
—L.C.

To my sweet son, Justice, who has been fighting leukemia this last year;
your laughter and courage make even the gloomiest days seem light.
You are my heart—I love you beyond words.
And to my ageless mother, the grandmother of all grandmothers, whose spirit inspires us all.
—J.W.

Our deepest thanks to Susan Raihofer, the finest agent around, and to the extraordinary minds and hearts who helped shape this book:

Jim Haner, Steven Goldstein, Lana Gersman, Franny O'Gorman and Jean Goldman, for their inspiration and ideas; Terri Augello, Jeff Robinson and Jeanine McLean-Griffin (Alicia Keys), Pippa Mills (Judy Blume), Carrie Potter (Steve Francis), and Bonnie Kramen (Olympia Dukakis), for help coordinating interviews; and to hair, makeup artists, and stylists Ashunta Sheriff, Nikki Tucker, Wouri Vice, and Susanna Burns.

A very special thanks to Sian Tom and MaryLeigh Krasniewisz for loaning us their time and great minds; to David Wong and Siena Tang for the beautiful prints; and to designer Maria Taffera Lewis, who makes us all look good.

This book would not exist were it not for the passion of Melanie Falick. Thanks to Anne Kostick, who so wisely guided its completion. Thanks to Betty Christiansen, and to Leslie Stoker and everyone at STC, for supporting the book through it all.

Finally, to the grandmothers who allowed us into their homes and lives and who brought to these pages their collective wisdom and grace— meeting you was this project's greatest reward.

To the friends who tended to my soul, my children, my dog, and these pages; thank you, Tina Way, Julie Henhapl, Chris Gilstrap, Linda Greenberg, Barbie Mahany, Tanya Barrientos, and especially Donna St. George, who gave me her mind and heart when mine were hard to find. Thanks also to Chicago's best writers' group for keeping my spot warm.

To my Aunt Ellie and my great, supportive circle of sisters; Stevi, Frannie, Marci, and especially Robin and Randi, whose advice—just finish the damn thing—was, as always, unparalleled. And to my mother-in-law, Saralee, who has taught me much about a grandmother's love and the resilience of the human heart.

Finally, thanks to my beautiful Avery, and to my son, Eric, thank you for your brilliant ideas (Steve Francis), endless curiosity (aren't you done yet), and the joy you bring all who know you. And to Jay, who gives me flight and a safe place to land.

—L.C.

Thank you to all my amazing assistants, especially Elise Ho, for organizing me; and to Piero Ribelli, grazie for your vision and for making me laugh.

We found guidance and comfort in the wisdom of doctors Zullo, Carroll, and Gardner, friends Anne Lamuniere, Siobhan Neary, and Joan Kuehl, all the staff at NYU, and everyone at Chai Lifeline. My thanks to my family, especially my step-daughters Gretchen, Heather and Shannon; to my two greatly missed grandmothers, Nana Sylvia and Nana Fan, to Dad, Jan and mother-in-law, Elizabeth. To my sister Holly, you are beautiful in every way. Also to Ellen Kiell, Susan Ronick and all my girlfriends who lent me their ears, shoulders and so much more.

And of course, to my husband and best friend, Hunter, a gentle soul whose love keeps me centered and is the most inspiring father I know. I love you more than Haagen Dazs.

—J.W.

Contents

Judy Blume & Elliot Blume . . . 10

Mable Wilson & Steve Francis . . . 18

Kathy O'Malley, Tris & Mick Bucaro,
Sara & Ian O'Malley . . . 24

Lydia Garcia, Shavon & Madison Ayala . . . 30

Vergeil DiSalvatore & Alicia Keys . . . 36

Adele Dolansky, Devon & Ryan Shircliff . . . 42

Bernice Wallis, Daniel, Samantha
& Matthew Libman . . . 46

Estella Wheeler . . . 52

Olympia Dukakis, Isabella, Sofia & Luka Zorich . . . 56

Ruth Slagle, Kristie Slagle Kienstra & Kelley Slagle . . . 60

Lillie Owens, Kendall & Mitchell Elie . . . 66

Gertrude Taylor . . . 70

Linda Davis, Ryan & Walter Davis,
Leslie Barmann, Sara & Christiaan Davis . . . 74

Mary Remini & Valerie Johnson . . . 80

Joan Logghe, Corina Logghe & Galen Haynes . . . 84

Rose Holtzman & Alexis Abramson . . . 88

Tawana Colon & Destiny Colon . . . 94

Hadassa Carlebach & Naftali Citron . . . 98

Corinne Gonzales & Stephanie Valdez . . . 104

Margaret Gray . . . 110

Rita Chopra, Leela & Tara Mandal . . . 114

Kimeng Ven & Jessica Nem . . . 118

Frances Sternhagen, Julia & Payton Carlin . . . 124

Introduction

Until recently, I did not give much thought to grandmothers or the role they play in our lives. My own grandmothers died before I could know them; one before I was born and the other shortly after. I think of them as a pastiche of snapshots and stories, two strong immigrants: my Grandma Yetta, with her love of the theater; my Grandma Faye, the bearer of my mother's large, graceful heart.

But these images and impressions, handed to me through others, were hardly enough to help me understand the magnitude of the relationship that I was about to explore. So as we began this project, I turned to the connections that were central to my life, and to which I'd devoted so much thought—my role as a daughter, a mother, a sister, a friend. If Jayne came to this project with thoughts of her beloved Nana Sylvia and Nana Fan, I came with the curiosity of a traveler who was about to see a great city that she'd only known through books.

Still, the word grandmother stirred a vague longing for something that my experiences and understanding of other relationships did not explain. Then, just as we were beginning this project, both of my parents died within the space of six months. I was in my mid-forties, a mother of two children, suddenly unmoored. My children had lost two of their grandparents: two people who, with a mere gaze, could tell them, "You are a miracle, the best of all that is possible in life." What I had begun with interest I turned to with new intensity.

Jayne and I wanted to find women of different backgrounds and outlooks, women who varied not only in who they are but also in how deeply the relationship defined them and the choices in their lives. Our aim was not to catalogue the role of grandmothers but to celebrate them through women of different perspectives.

Sifting through these profiles, I began to understand: Grandmothers give us access to worlds we don't know or can't see, connecting us to places and people or perceptions that widen the limits of our lives. They transport us through stories and language, but also through food and expressions and ordinary objects.

The very thing that distinguishes the relationship—the distance between the generations—is the heart of its mystery and strength. As a grandmother, Kathy O'Malley feels an abandon that she could never embrace as a harried, single mother. That distance gave Corinne Gonzales the ability to recognize her granddaughter Stephanie's untapped talent in a way that Stephanie's mother and Stephanie herself did not. It can grant a child a view beyond the cul-de-sac of a parent's perspective, as was the case for Rabbi Naftali Citron.

But perhaps the greatest mystery is the power of the attachment and what it conveys—a hunger to make sense of the world and our place in it.

In the year since my parents died, the stories and thoughts of the women gathered here have altered the way I look at my own loss, informed as I am by their humanity and their deep, affecting joy. In a society that celebrates youth, these women create intergenerational relationships of vital exuberance.

They guide us through these pages as only grandmothers can, cradling our awareness while directing our gaze, consoling us with their endurance, lengthening our pasts, inspiring even the most fearful among us to turn the page and go on.

It is hard to think of Judy Blume as a grandmother.
For starters, there's the name, blaring like a foghorn

from the island of adolescence. She is the voice of the twelve-year-old in her seminal book, *Are You There God? It's Me, Margaret*. She is the voice of Fudge, the beloved character known to anyone who has been to fourth grade lately.

She is an author who has sold so many books—more than 75 million—and whose characters are so imprinted in reader's minds, that her name alone transports even hardened adults to the soft tissue of teenage life.

But Judy Blume is also a sixty-six-year-old who has tended children, husbands, bills, and laundry, who's known birth and death and marriage and divorce. Her face is a blend of unvarnished youth (think Jessica Lange in the film *Tootsie*) and a world-wariness that comes with writing books that are both honored with the National Book Award and censored for her honest depiction of adolescent life.

She has one grandchild, her daughter Randy's son, Elliot. At twelve, Elliot is smack in the midst of the adolescent world that his grandmother has spent so much time imagining. That is why, perhaps, they seem divided less by generation than by gender. In this morning alone, the two of them have wrestled, mock fenced, traded barbs, thrown a ball, swung on a hammock. "I still am twelve years old inside, and I can put myself back there," Judy says. "I never think about it. It just comes out. It's something spontaneous. As I grow older, I guess I split in half

Judy Blume &
Elliot Blume

Elliot Blume and Judy Blume at her home on Martha's Vineyard.

because I see the world as the mother and the grandmother that I am, and I also can put myself back and identify totally with children."

The twosome moves from swing to hammock to wharf with the affection and mock disdain that comes so easily to teens who remember—even if from a distance—the feel of their grandmother's lap.

"I'm not allowed to hug him anymore," Judy explains as Elliot bobs and weaves, then covers his ears as she sings. "I'm not allowed to sing," she adds. "It's too embarrassing."

Elliot raises his eyebrows. "It's not embarrassing. You just can't sing."

"I can too sing!"

He shakes his head sadly. "No, Nonie. You can't."

Sally's Camp," as the compound here is known, is at the end of a winding dirt road, where wooded hillsides give way to postcard views. Tall trees, sail-dotted seas, and a soft blue horizon paint the backdrop of life in Martha's Vineyard. Judy writes in one of the three small cabins that accompany the main house (it's the one with the sign reading "Cuckoo"). Elliot was born the year Judy and her husband, George, bought the place. She remembers holding Elliot soon after his birth and feeling a connection so powerful that she took out a piece of paper then and there and wrote Elliot's name, the date, and "he's wonderful!"—as if an experience of that magnitude might slip away without documentation.

"I always come upon it when I'm cleaning out my desk, and it's this wonderful memory. I held him and I just really—I just felt this bond."

The first time Judy had Elliot on the Vineyard was just before his first birthday. Judy and George were renovating the main house at the Vineyard, and the three of them lived crammed into one of the small accompanying cabins. Thinking about that time now, Judy breaks into a grin at the sheer joy that Elliot brought to even the most mundane moments.

"I remember he was in a high chair, and we were singing and dancing, and he was just laughing—and you know, there's that wonderful sound when a baby throws back his head and is laughing, laughing out loud."

Ordinary outings became Elliot-inspired adventures. An auditorium became a hide-and-seek maze. "We'd pass some construction and we'd park there and he'd know every piece of equipment. He knew the name of every single truck. All you did was put him in a stroller and he was mesmerized."

Once, Judy went to awaken Elliot from a nap. "Did you see the pink truck, did you?" he asked excitedly. "It came through the window!"

The dream stuck with Judy, perhaps because she could—even then, in her late fifties—transport herself to the moment when a child doesn't yet distinguish between the real and a dream.

Since he was born, Elliot's been spending part of his summer with Judy at the Vineyard. She even installed a special seat in her kayak so they could paddle together. Once, as a preschooler, while kayaking with his grandmother, and as they came to shore he declared, "Someday, all of this will be mine!" Judy, slightly horrified, called her daughter, Randy, who reminded her mother that Elliot was not declaring his designs upon the place, but acting out a line from *The Lion King*.

She remembers holding him soon after his birth
and feeling a connection so powerful
that she took out a piece of paper then and there and wrote
Elliot's name, the date and "he's wonderful."

Together, they invented games. Elliot's favorite was the "Fudge game," in which Judy played Fudge, the four-year-old from *Tales of a Fourth Grade Nothing*, a book published in 1972. Even before Elliot could read, he'd memorized the Fudge books, carrying tapes of them everywhere he went. Randy bemoaned her fate as an adult daughter who could not escape her mother's voice. ("I told her to get him a headset," Judy offers.) In fact, it was Elliot who inspired Judy to bring Fudge back to the page. In 2002, she published *Double Fudge*, a book dedicated to Elliot.

"Of course I remember lots and lots with my own children," says Judy. "But Elliot came at a different time in my life. I'm different. You're at a time when you can just focus on this one wonderful thing. The relationship is different."

All morning, Judy has begged Elliot to put on sunscreen, to wear bug spray. Now, they are sitting on the grass in the sunshine, eye to eye. "Let's have a staring contest," Judy declares.

"Ready?" Elliot says. "Set, go."

Judy stares in Elliot's eyes but spots a fly circling his head. She thinks of ticks, of mosquitoes, of all the dangers that can hide in grasses.

"Nonie! You blinked five times. You can't blink in a staring contest."

"You didn't put on bug spray, did you?"

"Nonie! The point of a staring contest is to not blink."

Judy grabs the insect repellent and attempts to wipe it on Elliot, but he bats away her hand.

"I already have it on," he insists.

"You don't, do you? I see them coming in and out of your ears."

He sighs. "I'm charging them for hotel space."

I always thought I'd have lots of grandchildren around me," Judy says. "I always knew I was going to be a mother, always knew I wanted to have little children. I fantasized about that whole thing. But I came of age at such a different time."

Judy grew up in suburban New Jersey with a father who adored her and a mother who could be demanding and left Judy little room for rebellion. Her role, she knew from an early age, was to marry and raise a family in much the way she herself had grown up.

Judy headed to college just before the sexual revolution, when campuses were filled with young women like Judy who thought their route to freedom was through marriage. By the age of twenty-five, she'd married John Blume and had two young children. But she was deeply unhappy.

Her own father had died five weeks before her wedding. Throughout her twenties, Judy was sick often, raising two young children and finding freedom the only way she always had, through her imagination. As her children began school, Judy wrote feverishly until they were home, increasingly finding her voice on the page. Though she'd published a few stories and two books, it was the publication of *Are You There God?* in her early thirties that fueled her success and ambition.

The book stood out in part because of its subject matter: an honest depiction of female sexuality and Margaret's very personal relationship with God. But, told from the point of view of a twelve-year-old, it also stood as one of the few works of realistic fiction intended for young readers. It did not talk down to its audience but spoke to young girls in a way that even their mothers—*especially* their mothers—did not. If the book propelled Judy to significance, it also became the centerpiece of a bitter feud over censorship as right-wing groups battled to keep it and others of Judy's books off library shelves.

Among the book's most memorable characters was a grandmother, Sylvia Simon, who stood for the protagonist, Margaret, as an adult who understood her in a way her own parents did not. Sylvia was funny, fashionable, and defiant.

"I think she was the grandmother I thought I'd be someday," Judy says now. In creating Sylvia, Judy had imagined her as sixty, an age that seemed to her thirty-year-old self inordinately old. Judy's own grandmother died when she was fifteen, during the summer when she was at camp. Judy adored her grandmother and still despairs that her parents did not bring her home for the funeral.

"She was completely nonjudgmental," she says of her Nana. "Of course, I don't always take my own advice. But I think that's the role of grandparents.

"My mother, interestingly, I think, was a loving, nonjudgmental grandma to my children. But I thought she was judgmental with me. We had an intense relationship." Judy remembers appearing on television in the early years of her celebrity, wearing her mother's homemade sweaters, "surely not because that's what would be most becoming, but because it would please my mother."

When she was thirty-seven, she told her mother that she was divorcing John Blume. Her mother was devastated. "What will I tell my friends?" she wanted to know. Judy packed up her kids and moved away. "My husband and my mother were authority figures in my life, and I'd never rebelled as an adolescent. I would have never felt free enough to behave the way Elliot behaves."

It is lunchtime, and Judy pulls out whatever she has on hand—tuna, bread, celery, lettuce, tomatoes. "I get nervous before he comes and plan all these things and, of course, George tells me I try too hard." But she has learned from motherhood that the days that can seem so long when your children are little actually pass quickly. She savors the weeks with Elliot, especially because she fears that he will be her only grandchild.

She frets over whether he's eating right and whether he's had enough milk, and then she reminds herself that she is only with him for a few weeks every few months. "I tell myself, why should it matter if he's just had a Pepsi and he wants a root beer float?"

"Will you eat tuna if I make it?" she asks Elliot.

He shrugs.

"Yes?" she tries. "No?"

In *Are You There God?* Margaret watches her mother in the kitchen and sees not the woman she wants to be, but a woman who is opening and closing cabinets while smelling her armpits, checking to see if she needs deodorant. Judy thinks about this as she watches Elliot, reminds herself that he's at an age when adults are suddenly filled with flaws, when parents and grandparents seem to be leaking brain cells.

"Sometimes I find myself asking him questions and not even getting an answer. I find myself saying, 'Elliot, respond. Please.' "

For his part, Elliot is long past the point of reveling in his grandmother's celebrity. When asked how his Nonie is different from his mother, he shrugs and offers only, "My mother doesn't play home-run derby." His mother, Randy, is raising him on her own in Cambridge, Massachusetts, and is relaxed in her parenting style, allowing Elliot more latitude than his grandmother does when it comes to what he eats or the things he acquires. "I regret sometimes that I can't spoil him," Judy says, "that he seems to have everything he wants."

But what he wants—even at this age—is Judy.

As he was leaving for summer camp this year, he told Judy that she could write him twice a week. In previous summers, she'd written every day. But then just before he left for camp, he amended that request: "Two letters is the minimum," he told her.

One day during Elliot's visit, Judy found herself pressed into work, distracted by phone meetings about a movie version of her book *Deenie*. Two weeks later, she would learn that she had won the National Book Award, becoming the first author of books for young people to win this prestigious honor. But Elliot wasn't interested in the accolades or news of the film. All morning, he implored her to finish working.

"You promised," he reminded her. "You promised we'd spend the day together."

For Judy Blume, a writer who has faced down censors and critics, a woman who has battled the right wing and her mother's limiting expectations, there was nothing quite as satisfying as leaving behind adult demands so she could fall into step with Elliot and lose herself in his twelve-year-old world.

So there you are, a big-time NBA star, dribbling your way to stardom before a hometown crowd.

It's a near-perfect scene: you the conquering hero returning to Washington, D.C. once again to play against the Wizards. Your cousins are there. Your friends are there. And of course, your grandma's there. It could have been perfect (a perfect scene would not have allowed those turnovers, those bad passes). But now the game is over, and your grandma—the woman who still signals you from the stands, whose voice commands you even when she's not there—that grandma is headed your way. She's almost to the locker room when you realize that she's not coming to see you. No, she wants to see your new coach.

With most grandmothers, this would not be a big deal. But then Grandma Mable—as your friends, your teammates, even the security guards will attest—is not any grandma.

She gets right to the point. You've been in the NBA for a few years now and she knows that you've not been playing your best lately. The coach leans in, nodding, asking earnestly, "Do you have any advice for me, anything I should know about your grandson?"

As a matter of fact, she does. She tells him that he ought to stop yelling and hollering so much, running up and down the sidelines like that, he's going to get a heart attack. And then she thinks for a moment, thinks about your newfound fame, your life in Houston, surrounded by new friends and no family. She tells the coach to keep an eye on you. If the coach is taken aback, he doesn't show it. Instead, he shakes her hand warmly, smiles, says, anything else? She considers the question, then offers: "You could do something about his passing game."

Mable Wilson
& Steve Francis

Mable Wilson and Steve Francis
on the deck of her home
in Silver Springs, Maryland.

By the standards of sports stars and the agents who represent them, this rates as one of the more unusual intersections of a player's professional and personal lives. But in the world of Steve Francis and his grandmother, Mable Wilson, this is ordinary fare.

To ESPN regulars, Steve is known as "the Franchise," one of the post-Jordan generation of basketball players who has the star power to generate headlines and inspire fans. At 6' 3", he's distinguished not by his size but by his speed and his vertical leap, his dazzling form of play. In his first year as point guard for the Houston Rockets, he was the Co-Rookie of the Year and led the team in scoring, assists and steals, pulling off a trifecta that is almost never seen in a rookie.

As Steve's grandmother, Mable is both force and anchor, an orienting beacon in a world of dizzying dimensions. Anyone who deals with Steve deals with Mable. This means his agent, his friends, and, as she makes certain, anyone who wants to be his coach. Pity the poor soul who might be an adversary.

"Wheeew boy, I tell you," Steve deadpans when thinking of her role in his life. "She's got my back."

By its very nature, a grandparent's relationship to a child is an imbalance of power. But as an adult who stands 5'7", Mable looms especially large. When Steve was eighteen, his mother, Mable's daughter Brenda, died, and it was Mable who helped him face his greatest fears and answer to his better self. Mable was central to his sizeable achievements. "My grandmother Mable gave us everything," he said, referring to his family when talking to reporters in 1999. "She gave us the love, support, and balance that we needed."

What Steve has given his grandmother in return—a grand house, his winning jersey, his most prized trophies—has not shifted the balance between them. These are mere emblems, returns on an alliance of intangible proportions.

"She's my momma's momma, and you sense that, even as a kid," Steve says. "She's someone who feels the same as your mother, only she's lived longer, and maybe that gives her more perspective."

Steve loved balls, even as a baby, even before he could talk. He'd bobble them with his feet until he could stand and bounce them with his hands. He was born into a home where his father was absent but his mother ran a tight ship. And while all the kids looked to Mable as a second mother, Steve was with her the most. "Of all of us—and there were like twenty-four grandchildren—she was hardest on me," he says, shaking his head. "I don't know why." Mable can tell you why. She's raised six kids and became mother to Steve and his three siblings, plus adopted nine of the other grandchildren, eight of whom still live with her. She can see even in their earliest choices in their small failures and successes, the potential that will shape their lives. In Steve, Mable saw talent, but also that ineffable quality that drives kids through discouragement and pain to achieve greatness.

"You know, some of the kids are the ones you have to pull out of bed," Mable says. "They get shot down once and won't go back and try again. Steve was the first kid to have a job in the neighborhood, and then he wanted to get all of his friends jobs. People were just drawn to him."

As Steve's grandmother, Mable is both force and anchor,
an orienting beacon in a world
of dizzying dimensions.
Anyone who deals with Steve deals with Mable.

He wanted to play football. But he was small, and by age thirteen he was pouring his determination and ambition into basketball. Every day, he'd measure himself against inch marks on his mother's wall, waiting for the growth spurt his grandmother promised would come. His pronouncement that he was going to be the next Michael Jordan was no different than that of legions of kids for whom such statements are akin to buying a lottery ticket. But this was a kid who did not give up. After school, he'd head to the local Boys Club, where he caught the eye of famed coach Tony Langley. On summer nights, when he couldn't sleep, he'd sneak out to play ball until dawn, an act that would draw swift punishment from his mother. His grandmother took him aside. "For heaven's sake, Steve," she told him. "If you're going to sneak out, don't bounce the ball on the way home."

By the time he was a senior in high school, Steve seemed destined to play ball, at least in college if not in the pros. But in 1996, Brenda—Steve's mother—died of cancer. "I felt as though I'd lost the right side of me," Mable says. His mother's death stripped Steve of certainty about his future, about his place in the world. "I never even knew anyone whose parents had died and never thought of it as something that could happen to me."

With Steve's mother gone, Mable feared that he'd leave school for good and turn to friends and influences that would destroy him. He'd never been away from home and was reluctant even to look at a school away from home if that meant leaving what he'd known. She knew, too, that she had to tread carefully: Steve couldn't be pushed. Mable turned to Tony Langley, Steve's basketball coach from the Boys Club. Together, they searched out colleges, gathered together Steve's records, completed his paperwork and pushed Steve to go to a preparatory school in Connecticut and then to San Jacinto Junior College in Texas.

"It wasn't like she left me alone, but she talked to me and wanted to see how I'd react," Steve says. "She let me know that I had a choice—that I could make this a blessing and do something positive with my life."

But he was miserable living so far away. He transferred twice and finally landed at the University of Maryland, where he had a stellar year and led the basketball team to its most successful season. By that time, he had the strength to face down a different kind of danger—the kind that comes with fame, success, and sudden wealth.

It is a hot Sunday in June, and Steve gathers with the rest of the family to celebrate his cousin Tahjuan's high school graduation. Mable has cleaned the already-clean house, filled the fridge with soda, fruit, and platters of sandwiches, posted signs on doors warning her grandkids that they are not to mess up the guest bathroom, that they are to leave their shoes outside.

Mable takes a seat at the kitchen table, and removes her shoes, the only sign that after raising some nineteen kids—six of her own, the nine grandkids she adopted, plus Steve and his two siblings (the others were already adults), plus keeping tabs on fifteen great grandchildren—she might be tiring. In addition to losing Brenda, Mable lost another daughter to drugs and addiction. That daughter had nine children and Mable knew that if she didn't adopt them, they'd end up in foster care. Mable's own mother was dying at the time and urged her to keep the family together.

"Some days I am so tired, just so tired, and I pray for patience—patience most of all," she says. "But each day I get up and thank God for the day I had and the day I'm about to have. I am truly, truly blessed."

For his siblings and cousins, Steve's arrival is extra reason for celebration. But this is Tahjuan's day; Mable makes sure of that. She watches as Tahjuan greets every visitor with a firm handshake and a wide grin. As one and then another of the grandchildren pass by, Mable introduces each one, noting some special talent or accomplishment: Tahjuan's award-winning art; Michelle's basketball prowess.

When Steve walks in, he elicits the same "Hey, Steve, honey" that Mable bestows on the other kids. He bends over, kisses her on the cheek. "I just love these kids," Mable says. "You know, my oldest daughter tells me I'm easier on them, that this is a different era and they're different. I say, 'How are they any different? They bleed. They cry. They're kids just like you were.'"

Steve's first mission upon signing his contract was to buy his grandma a larger house. He describes this not as a choice, but a clear obligation for anyone in his shoes. It was a heady time for Steve. Sportswriters were touting his arrival. The boy who had cherished his first paycheck of $175.17 (Mable kept it) was signing a contract for millions.

Mable had her own vision of what this home would be. She picked a place where she felt comfortable, an older home in an edgy neighborhood. Steve had just bought his own first home, and flush with that experience, he was certain, upon seeing his grandmother's choice, that she was making a big mistake. But Mable wasn't looking for an investment. She was looking for a home.

"See, I just wanted to be happy, and I wasn't going to have anyone telling me what to do," she says.

Steve came to talk with her, to set her straight. Mable saw him coming.

"It was the first time he'd ever raised his voice to me," she says. Mable remembers rising to her feet and jabbing Steve with her finger so that he fell back into her rocking chair. "I told him, 'You know, Steve, I love you to death. But I don't care how much money you make. You can have it coming out of your eyes, your ears, and your nose, and I'm still gonna be your grandma. I don't need your approval for anything. Not yet, anyway.'"

She is talking from the home they eventually agreed upon, a grand five-bedroom house in suburban Silver Springs with a spiral staircase and soaring ceilings. On the fireplace mantel and along the walls are evidence of Steve's triumphs: trophies, medallions, large photographs.

Mable remembers the first time she saw him play professionally. She could not travel to Texas, but even at home, connected via satellite, Mable could feel the weight of his accomplishment, the sheer excitement both of them felt as he soared to extraordinary heights. "He's your grandson, but you see him and think, He's amazing. This was his dream, and he made it happen."

But if she's the keeper of his legacy, she's also a not-so-distant conscience. Once, while watching him play on TV, she saw him and a teammate erupt in frustration. "You boys need to watch your mouths," she told him when he called her after the game.

"You couldn't have heard me," he protested.

"Honey, I can read your lips. At least turn away from the camera."

At the same time, the distance pains her. He is young and she worries about the people who surround him, the friendships and associations that come with wealth and fame. One night in his first professional year, she was awakened by a phone call from a stranger who wanted to know her reaction to the news that Steve had been stopped while driving and arrested. Mable doesn't drive, but that night she was ready to jump into her car and head for Houston. A phone call convinced her that he was fine, that there was no merit to the charges, which were dropped; he was resolving the situation without her.

"When I talked to him, I calmed down," she says. "There are always going to be people who want to harm him. That's the world he's in. All I can do is pray."

In 2004, Steve was traded to the Orlando Magic, leaving behind a home he'd come to love, friendships with the likes of Rockets center Yao Ming, and a program he'd built for neighborhood kids. The move was hard for him. But Mable reminded him that he loves what he does, that he is well paid for his job. When he talked of his reservations, his grandmother repeated a mantra: "Remember where you came from, and you'll never lose your bearings."

Leaning against each other on the deck of Mable's home, they are nearly eye-to-eye. Steve wraps one arm around his grandmother and holds a basketball in the other. "Someday, I'll show you how to use this," he deadpans, twirling the basketball on his finger.

No amount of money, fame, and trophies will tip the scales that balance both their lives. Mable leans back far enough so that he can catch her grin. "Steve, honey," she says, nodding toward the ball. "I already know."

Kathy O'Malley,
Tris & Mick Bucaro,
Sara & Ian O'Malley

Beneath a flight path, along an industrial entrance
to O'Hare Airport, a blond woman of indeterminate age

pulls up in a car near a sign that says, "No Parking, Standing, or Waiting." There she parks her car, stands, and waits. Next to her are her grandsons, Tris and Mick. In a million years, she would never have imagined that she would be where she is at this moment in her life, a grandmother with time enough to watch planes soar by. Hell, she didn't think she'd survive motherhood—or that her kids would survive her parenting.

The woman, Kathy O'Malley, is best known as half of *Kathy and Judy*, a Chicago radio talk show so successful it has spawned CDs, chat rooms, and conferences. But at this moment, she can barely hear her own voice. Tris spots the plane first, the descending hulk of a 727. It buzzes the suburban rooftops, banks toward O'Hare. This is what they came for, this plane-dazed euphoria. First comes the roar, then the vibration. She folds her grandsons in her arms and they feel it together—a shot straight to the heart.

On the steps in Kathy O'Malley's courtyard
in Chicago, Illinois (left to right):
Ian O'Malley, Kathy O'Malley, Tris Bucaro,
Sara O'Malley, and Mick Bucaro.

"You hear you're going to be a grandmother, and you think, *Oh, how nice*. But you have no idea," Kathy says. She is a small, compact woman who feels most comfortable in overalls and gardening gloves. Fans meet her and say, "I feel like I know you." This is in part because radio is intimate in a way that television and print are not. But it's also because Kathy and co-host Judy Markey, whose fans call them and one another "girlfriend," talk with listeners as if they are chatting around the kitchen table. Topics run the gamut, from sexuality to red peppers, but mostly the discussions center on the relationships that define women's lives. No subject is sacred, not Kathy's marriage and divorce, nor the years when her daughter had an eating disorder and her son spent less time at his school than Kathy did.

"There's this 'grandma mind-set' that some people have, and they see their job as a grandparent is to impart wisdom. That attitude is, 'I've lived so long and know so much and I'm here to impart wisdom.' Well, the truth is, I don't know squat. I know what got me here, and I don't think I have wisdom to impart to my grandchildren. But I love the heck out of them, and that is my job—to love them so much that they squirm. They are a joy unlike anything I've known."

In the late 1970s, Kathy was in a bad marriage, and a dead-end job, her spirits buoyed only by a number—the amount of money that would allow her to leave her husband and give her kids a stable life. She didn't have much in the way of job experience or higher education. But she did have good friends, one of whom worked at the *Chicago Tribune* and knew that Aaron Gold, the paper's society columnist, was in need of a new assistant.

She started as Gold's secretary, working hard to make the job a success, but fearful, too, of what her absence meant for her kids. "Every minute you're thinking, *Am I doing this right? How much am I hurting them?* The stress is never-ending."

By the time Gold died in 1983, Kathy was his obvious successor. For the next decade, she wrote six columns a week, feature stories as often as twice a week, and even hosted occasionally on radio programs. It was both thrilling and draining, a fairy-tale job with nightmarish hours. There was never enough time, never enough money, and she seemed never to be in the right place at the right time. Her children were teenagers, bruised from the divorce, often alone both literally and psychologically, with few friends who understood what their lives felt like.

Kathy's son, Patrick, was struggling at school, skipping classes, probably drinking, maybe worse. What she didn't know was that her daughter, Colleen, was struggling too, battling bulimia and a depression so severe she would eventually be hospitalized.

One day Patrick ducked out of school and went for a joyride in Kathy's car, which might have gone unnoticed had Patrick not crashed head-on with a truck carrying sheets of plate glass. Too young to have a license, he panicked and left the scene.

"I got a call from my ex, and he's saying, 'Patrick's been arrested for a hit-and-run. What the hell is going on? Why are you such a crappy mother?' Meanwhile, I had to pull $900 out of nowhere, and I had to find a way for him to take responsibility for this."

As a grandmother, she has the luxury of dwelling in their world without the competing demands. . . She has something she says she only acquired after her children had grown—the certitude that kids will make mistakes, will do stupid things and go through hard times, but ultimately they will be OK.

To pay it back, Patrick took the only job he could get, at Burger King. Kathy remembers watching Patrick one night from a distance as he flipped hamburgers onto a grill; the image still cuts so deeply her eyes fill up just remembering it. "I watched this child, this six-foot, sixteen-year-old child, put burgers on this rolling thing into the grill and I went out to my car and just cried."

The September night is hot and humid, and there's a languor in the air, evening stretched as far as a school night will allow. In front of Kathy's apartment building there is a courtyard—a small stretch of grass, gardens, and sidewalk enclosed on three sides. For Kathy and her grandkids, this is extended living space. A few days earlier, while gardening with her grandsons, Kathy encouraged them to dig holes so deep and wide they could fit inside them.

Colleen watches from the sidelines. Like her mother, she is divorced, raising two children on her own. But Colleen, who works for a Chicago advertising agency, lives in a world that is far more accepting of her role than the one her mother knew. Patrick is now a technology professional with his wife, Ikuko, and two children. "They've both turned out to be such lovely, lovely people, wonderful parents," Kathy marvels. "Just the

other day, I was talking to my daughter, and I said I don't feel like I was that good a mom because I was so busy. I wasn't there when they needed me. And she said, 'The one thing is, Mom, you showed up. Every day. You were there.'"

Now that Kathy's a grandmother, Patrick and Colleen see in her a person they'd not known as children, a grandmother who not only has time and resources but wants more than anything to dwell in the world where their children are. "How hasn't she changed?" Patrick laughs.

At the moment, Kathy is on her hands and knees drawing a hopscotch grid while Tristan advises her on the correct dimensions for Sky Blue. As he hovers, he opens his mouth wide enough for his grandma to see a tooth that is dangling, just ready to fall. She stops drawing for a moment so she can offer up the appropriate response: "Oooohhh, yech!" Hearing this, Mick and her granddaughter, Sarah, climb on Kathy to get a better view, debating the grossest ways they can think of to remove a tooth. It is then, when the three of them are upon her, that they all hear the barely audible but unmistakable sound of a child passing gas, a sound that sends Kathy and the kids into fits of laughter.

"Oh my God, Mick, you are the king of farts," she tells her grandson, to much delight.

"I thought you said I was the king of farts," Tris protests.

"You're awfully good. But I think you have competition." They are rolling on the ground now, overcome with giggles as Colleen and Patrick take it all in from the side.

"We're very, very lucky to have her," Colleen says. "She gives them so much—material things, things I can't afford to give them. Like, Tris is interested in the presidency, so she took him to Washington, D.C. But she also gives them herself. Sometimes, I'll watch them together, and she just becomes overwhelmed, she loves them so much, and they feel this sense of security. I think I knew even as a kid that she was a cool mom, that she didn't do things like all the other moms, and I think my kids get a lot out of that, too. She's impulsive and fun."

Patrick's daughter, Sarah, loves coming to Grandma's, where she can stand on the table or run through the room, acts she knows would get her into trouble at home.

Kathy loves this. "When they're your own children, you're constantly thinking, *Did I do this right? Should I have done this differently? Are they going to turn out OK?*"

As a grandmother, she has the luxury of dwelling in their world without the competing demands of work, home, and self. She has something she says she only acquired after her children had grown—the certitude that kids will make mistakes, do stupid things, and go through hard times, but ultimately they will be OK.

"People would tell me that, but I couldn't believe it as a parent," she says. "When you're a mom, oh my God, it's so stressful and so hard."

Kathy wants to offer these children a place where they will feel safe, where they won't be judged, and where they can say *fart* with impunity.

Once, while speaking at a conference made up mostly of retirees, Kathy talked about the distinction between the fun grandma—the one who gets on her hands and knees with the kids—and the grandmother who relates best to her grandkids across a table. When she asked which in the room were the "fun" grandmas, just about every hand went up. "We all want to think of ourselves as the one the kids want to be with," she says.

"I sometimes feel like I was this terrible mom," she says. "I was working twelve hours a day. I was so poor. We had next to no money. My kids had to plan four weeks ahead to buy blue jeans." The thought of standing with her kids at O'Hare and watching planes pass overhead would have struck her as the height of absurdity.

"Oh my God," she says throwing her head back laughing. "Who had the time?"

Now, as the evening winds down in Kathy's courtyard, Sarah asks if she can stay overnight with Grandma the way Tris and Mick do. "You think you're ready for that?" Kathy asks, delighted. Sarah throws her arms around Kathy, and then the other kids pile on, the lot of them giggling so hard they don't bother looking up as a plane passes overhead.

Though her granddaughters have not yet arrived,
Lydia Garcia is drawn outside as if by some invisible charge,

some undetectable shift in the Old Taos air that tells her they are coming. This is how it is with Lydia and her granddaughters. They keep in touch with the usual methods: letters, phone calls, visits. Then there are the more spiritual routes. When in different time zones or different countries, they synchronize their watches so they know the exact time to pray.

Lydia Garcia is a santera, a painter of saints. Her work can be found in the homes of friends and celebrities, in out-of-the-way stores, and in the Smithsonian Institution. They are deeply spiritual works, made of passion and signed with a prayer.

Lydia's relationship with her grandchildren is built much the same way, so indelibly woven into her soul that when they are apart, she feels their absence like a phantom limb.

"I can't separate what is inside me from the love I feel for them. It is the love I feel for my children made deeper, the love I feel for God. They are an extension of that love, and there is a lot of power in that—a lot of power."

Their arrival on this Saturday is cause for celebration. Lydia lives in Taos, New Mexico, in the same adobe home her grandparents built. Shavon and Madison are sixteen and thirteen and live in Albuquerque.

Lydia Garcia, Shavon & Madison Ayala

Madison Ayala, Lydia Garcia, and Shavon Ayala walking in the cemetery near Lydia's home in Ranchos de Taos, New Mexico.

They are teenagers with demanding schedules and expectations, part of a world Lydia never knew. But ever since the girls were little, they shared a closeness with their grandmother that even their mother finds hard to describe.

"They're more like sisters," Ana Medina Ayala says. "There's something between them that you don't see too often."

Now, when Lydia sees the girls, she calls to them, "My beautiful babies!" There are hugs and kisses and much to-do about the loveliness of Shavon's hair, the shortness of Madison's skirt.

"So, you heard from your friend Dave?" Lydia asks Shavon, picking up on last visit's news of an angry split between the young people. The three have settled around a small wooden table covered with brushes and paints and pieces of wood. They pick up brushes as naturally as they would reach for salt. It is what they've always done.

Madison eyes Shavon's work. "Hers is so good."

"This is not a competition," Lydia reminds them. "Yours is good for you; hers is good for her. It's from what's inside you.

"You know," she says, turning back to Shavon's relationship, "you have to forgive or forget. Because if you don't forgive, your body knows it. You'll get cataracts or arthritis or something. As much as you think it should happen to his body, it will happen to yours."

Shavon smiles at this. "I've decided to forgive him."

"And you know," Lydia says, "you don't have to be so serious. It's too young to be so serious."

This is their routine. When the girls were little, they would sleep in

Lydia's bed, staying up late telling stories. Sometimes they cooked or watched movies or went with Lydia to church. But always they painted. They'd take hold of a paintbrush and with it, a legacy.

"I tell them all the time: Feed the soul and the rest is easy," Lydia says. "My babies, they don't know what it's like to suffer for everything, to fight for every little thing. They are so blessed and have so much. They say, 'I know, Grandma, I know.' But I don't think they can know. My hope is to give them that—not so that they struggle, but so they know they have to do it because they are one of us, so that they can be true to who they are."

As a child, Lydia did not have choices. She was the oldest of five girls. Her father did not have an education, but he taught himself to read. As a carpenter and carver, he built art into the girls' lives. Without money for pencils or paints, he read to his daughters from the Bible, and Lydia would use charcoal from the stove to draw what she heard. "Just remember," he would say. "You can travel anywhere in books."

Lydia grew up to believe that with the mind, the will, and belief in God, you could do anything. Her mother sewed and took care of a nearby family and their little girl. And when Lydia finished sixth grade, she too went to work at this family's home, caring for the little girl, cleaning the chicken coop, seeing for the first time that there were lives very different from her own.

It was in this home that Lydia met her first artists. The father was a painter, and Lydia learned that art could feed more than the soul. She would return home with remnants of paint and oilcloths and dreams. "I didn't understand that he was an artist," she says of her employer, "but I could tell there was something different that I was drawn to." Over time, she had other jobs. She worked in a hospital, for a model, for a hairstylist. She imagined herself a nurse, a model, cutting hair. But these were her "faraway dreams."

She knew what reality had in store for her. At sixteen, she married a man who would come and go from her life for the next six years. By twenty-two, she was a single mother with four young children and a sixth-grade education.

On her own with her children, Lydia earned her high school diploma and eventually opened a hair salon, which became a mainstay of the neighborhood. When times were tight, she'd go door to door selling homemade potholders. Always, she painted. But art was, something she did to feed her spirit. In her mid-thirties, she remarried, became pregnant, and saw that her life would become easier. But ten months after she married, she and her husband were in a car accident that killed her husband and left Lydia crippled for three years. The baby—a girl—died.

"It was a terrible, terrible time," she says.

Her art sustained her. She signed up for an art class, but the teacher discouraged her from taking it, worried that she'd lose the spontaneity in her work. Occasionally, she'd sell one of her pieces, supplementing her haircutting income, and little by little, her work gained notice. Then in the late 1970s, Lydia found a lump on her neck—a terrifying moment that would prove to inspire her as an artist. Surgery proved that the lump was benign, but it left her unable to hold up her arms for long periods of time, a necessity if she was to cut hair. It was God's way, she figured: It was time to turn her life over to her art.

Lydia's oldest son—Madison and Shavon's father, Anthony Ayala—has always been her biggest supporter. "We grew up together," Lydia explains. She put him through college, and he was determined to repay her. To get enough money for law school, he sold one of her pieces, but soon discovered that the pieces sold themselves.

"He's the one who built this studio," Lydia says proudly.

By the time Shavon and Madison were born, she was an established artist. Shavon and Madison's mother, Ana, remembers that when the girls were little and visiting their grandmother, they'd all sneak out of bed in the middle of the night to go paint, which is how Ana would find them in the morning.

Now, when Shavon and Madison hear friends talk of their grandmothers, they see the rolled eyes, the *what a drag to spend a weekend with your grandmother,* and they realize how lucky they are to have a relationship that they rely on and that draws them into a world outside of their own.

"I think we speak differently, like we have a different language," Shavon says. "She teaches us through her art, through her spirituality, through church, through the prayers that she puts on the backs of her paintings. It's different than with anyone else. She understands us."

They talk about everything, from the last movie they rented—*Legally Blonde*—to what it means to pray, to the death of Madison's beloved dog Caesar. Lydia painted a picture of Caesar and insisted that Madison do the same. She had her write poems and stories so that the dog's spirit would be with her always.

Now, as daylight fades, Madison and Shavon walk down a crumbling street that leads from Lydia's home to a nearby cemetery. There is a soft wind rustling trees and, beyond that, the faint call of evening birds. They walk among the graves, pointing to where Lydia buried her mother and father, where her grandparents are buried as well. Lydia brings the girls here as a reminder, as if to say, "Here. This is a part of you. This is where you're from."

Soon, the girls too will leave, returning to their lives in Albuquerque, to their friends and cheerleading and work toward college. They will, Lydia knows, move on.

But earlier this month, Shavon, her new license in hand, drove with Madison to surprise Lydia. They knocked on her door, saying, "Get ready, Grandma, we're taking you to dinner."

"Where's your mama?" Lydia said, searching through the doorway.

"We're here alone!" The girls were nearly bursting with excitement.

Lydia could not believe it. "No, no. That can't be, that the babies can drive all by themselves?" Lydia said with mock horror. But in her mind, she noted with delight that at this milestone of independence, they'd come running to her.

All Alicia Keys wanted was to find a gift for her grandmother.

Her nana has always been central to her life,

the person who, with a single word or hug, can still the noise of everyday life.

From her childhood growing up in New York City to her graduation at age sixteen from the Professional Performing Arts School (she was valedictorian) to the release of her chart-topping album, Alicia found her voice in a world where it can be hard to hear yourself think.

"I can be on the road for months and months, and all I need is some Nana time," Alicia says. "The simple act of reaching out to her, to say, 'Hi, how are you,' to say nothing—just the sound of her voice has really saved me at times. She just brings me back, gives me a sense of peace."

But when it comes to thanking Nana, Alicia has struggled to find the right gift. Her nana is a private woman, so private that many of her friends and neighbors don't know that her granddaughter is Alicia Keys. She is a retired nurse and a tireless volunteer at her local elementary school on Long Island. She has a comfortable home and the resources to get what she needs. What Vergeil DiSalvatore values most is her anonymity because it offers a haven where Alicia the star can be Alicia her granddaughter.

But in 2001, of all years, Alicia wanted to do something special for her nana. Her first album, *Songs in A Minor*, had won five Grammy Awards and sold fifteen million copies worldwide. She was celebrated on *Oprah*, by *People* magazine, by critics who marveled at the depth and range of her work. Surely, she could come up with something that her grandma wanted, something Nana wouldn't buy for herself.

Vergeil
DiSalvatore
& Alicia Keys

Alicia Keys and Vergeil DiSalvatore
at Alicia's mother's
New York City apartment.

Vergeil thought about the kids in her school and how they would probably never get to meet someone like Alicia. The kids were preparing for a spring concert; perhaps Alicia could come see it. Vergeil didn't ask Alicia to perform, she just wanted her to be there, to meet the kids. There was one stipulation: Alicia and Vergeil agreed that only the principal and superintendent should know the name of the surprise guest.

Alicia was delighted. The day of the concert, she'd had an hour of sleep and had just returned from an overseas tour. She arrived at the school with an armload of signed photographs.

"The night before the concert, she signed hundreds of autographs so that each of the kids could have one," Vergeil says, her voice cracking. She is sitting next to Alicia and describing that day, she can barely get the words out. "When you talk about big moments, there have been so many. She sang at Radio City Music Hall. She won the Grammys. She was valedictorian. But I think seeing her there that day." She shakes her head, blinking back tears.

Although Vergeil's son, Craig Cook, and Alicia's mother lived apart, he wanted his parents to become involved in his daughter's life. "Here's this big guy with this tiny little baby, no bigger than his forearm," Vergeil remembers. "I told him, 'The moment you present her to me, she is my grandchild. I don't care what you do. She is in my life forever.' "

Alicia's mother, Terri Augello, was then a twenty-nine-year-old of Italian-English descent. She is as outgoing as Alicia's grandmother is quiet. But they share a strength that has instructed Alicia throughout her life. And both knew that Alicia was born with prodigious gifts.

From her mother, Alicia acquired a fiery passion for the arts, a brazen belief in self-expression. From her grandmother, she says she learned the power of quietude, and the grace that comes from empathy. "She's such a feeling person, and she gets inside people's lives," Alicia says, holding Nana's hand. "That ability to relate and feel compassion for others; that's something I definitely get from her."

The two adult women took pains to give Alicia a sense of home that extended from her mother's place in Manhattan to her grandmother's house on Long Island. "The package has left," Terri would tell Vergeil when Alicia departed for her grandmother's. And in turn, Vergeil would call to say, "The package has arrived."

Alicia succeeded at whatever she did. She was a talented swimmer and dancer, a quick student. Within two years of starting piano lessons at age five, Alicia was playing Chopin sonatas. By age fourteen she'd written her first song.

She graduated at sixteen with a scholarship to Columbia University and a teenager's certainty that her mother didn't understand who she needed to be. She wanted to be on her own, but with a recording contract in hand, she wondered whether college was where she belonged. In making that decision, as with so many others in her life, she ran through her options with her grandmother, searching for advice.

"I go to her and say, 'What should I do?'" Alicia says. "And she'll say, 'I'll give you my two cents. It's your dollar, but here's my two cents.'"

The early days of her career proved painful. Alicia was fighting to be heard in an industry that had its own formula for how Alicia was to be sold. Every step seemed protracted, every move headed in the wrong direction. She'd call her grandmother, and even when she wasn't talking about the business, about her fears and worries, her grandmother knew just what to say.

"You know how there are moments when you hear something and it just puts everything into perspective?" Alicia says. "That's what she did for me. She just said to me, 'Nothing before its time.' And somehow, when she said it, everything just clicked."

As Alicia's fame has grown, so has her longing for "Nana time," a need so palpable that even her crew knows it when they see it. Sometimes, she'll call just to hear her grandmother's voice. Other times, her hunger is more literal. "We were in Europe, the last week of the tour, and I called her. I said, 'Nana. I'm starving. They're not feeding me.' There was no good food out there and just to be able to tell her what I wanted—'can I have some soup, some fish, sweet potatoes, and broccoli.'"

"And baked apple," her nana says.

"And baked apple. And just saying that—I had one more show to do and it made me feel so much better."

When the principal at Vergeil's school introduced their special guest at the school's spring concert, the auditorium erupted in ecstatic applause and cheers. Alicia spoke to the kids, spoke from the heart without notes but with an authenticity that moved her grandmother to tears.

"Won't you sing for us?" one of the children asked after Alicia fin-

ished talking with them. "Well, I can't sing for you," Alicia told them. "But I can sing with you." With that, she sat down at the piano, and together the auditorium did a rousing rendition of her hit single "*Fallin'*."

Vergeil, in the front row, could barely speak. "I leaned over to my friend, and I said, 'Wow. That's my granddaughter.'"

For Alicia, the moment was a great achievement.

"You know, you just want to shower her with all this appreciation," she says of her grandmother, "and when it comes to her birthday or Christmas, we just pull our hair out. So to be able to go to the school. We started singing together, and they started singing my song, and it was this big, big moment for me. She was just sitting there smiling, and it made me so happy. To make her happy, that's everything."

It's been several months since Alicia's second album, *The Diary of Alicia Keys,* was received with acclaim. When she asked her nana to be in a book about grandmothers, Vergeil at first declined.

"I absolutely did not want to do it, did not want to give up my anonymity. I didn't think it was the right thing to do," she says. But Alicia pulled out all the stops, telling her nana that she deserved to be celebrated, that Alicia wanted people to know the role she'd played in her life. When that didn't convince her, Alicia pulled out a trump card. "I told her that this was for my grandchildren, so one day they'd know what she meant to me."

"Yep," Vergeil laughs. "That did it." She wipes her tears, proclaiming that it's a good thing they already had their photo session: Her makeup is ruined.

"Oh Nana," Alicia says, hugging her. "You are so beautiful."

Oh the difference a generation can make.

Adele Dolansky, Devon & Ryan Shircliff

Twenty years after she changed the face of soccer, Adele Dolansky is the model of grandmotherly restraint. She cheers on her granddaughter from the sidelines without a hint of the fiery rhetoric that defined her as the woman who gave girls the chance to play the game.

"My grandma is the nicest person in the world," ten-year-old Devon proclaims. "She'll always make me feel great and tell me, 'Even if you stink, you're still great in my eyes.'"

This is the Adele Dolansky who hounded soccer officials, prodded politicians, argued, lobbied, and yelled so that girls' soccer would have the same respect and resources enjoyed by boys.

With a few choice phrases ("What kind of bullshit is this?" was a favorite), she helped transform youth soccer in Virginia, Maryland, and Washington, D.C., and built a girls' soccer program that caught fire around the nation. She brought the same aggressive competitiveness to the task of coaching her daughter Michelle's team.

Today, her daughter is the coach and Adele, as grandma, is a kinder, gentler (though still competitive) fan. "Devon and I are the ones at odds now, and Grandma's there to comfort Devon, to help her deal with dealing with me," Michelle says.

Now in her early sixties, Adele's been dubbed "the Grandmother of Girls' Soccer," a woman whose outrage and persistence paid off for future generations of players. The resources that her granddaughters have come to

Devon Shircliff, Adele Dolansky, and Ryan Shircliff in the backyard in Fairfax, Virginia.

43

expect—well-groomed fields, uniforms, training that could lead to competitive play—were almost unheard-of when Adele's daughter began to play the game.

"In the beginning, it was like, 'Oh, you want referees too? The field wasn't enough?' " Adele remembers. She was then a stay-at-home mother in suburban Virginia. She'd already signed up her son to play soccer. Two years later, she did the same for her daughter and, at the same time, volunteered to coach.

But where her son had played in an organized league, the girls were expected to play in the fringes, in time slots and on fields that were not being used by the boys. The girls could not even have their own uniforms. They were expected to borrow dirty shorts and shirts from the boys, which they washed to wear and then washed again to return in time for the boys to play. "Imagine the message that sends—having to wear some other kids' dirty uniforms. Like our girls had nothing better to do than wash the boys' laundry." Adele's words become hard and deliberate, her voice gaining fury at the memory of those days.

In 1977, Adele took over as president of the fledgling Washington Area Girls Soccer League (WAGS). Seasons were arranged on her basement floor; pieces of paper matched players and teams with fields and time slots. Players donated their spare time to raise money for the league and build the WAGS tournament. "There was a sense that we were all low on the totem pole," Adele says. "We all had a need to prove ourselves."

One day, in 1979, Adele learned that Maryland was planning a state cup for boys but did not have one for girls. Adele hounded the state association board of directors. She popped up at meetings, demanded floor

time, refused to accept their assurances that a tournament was in the works. "Their response was always that it takes time, that we needed to be patient. It was an approach of, 'Oh, let's find a way to pacify you.' "

Adele had her own approach. She challenged Maryland to offer something concrete in the way of a girls' tournament or she'd "pack the lobby with 3,000 pissed-off little girls in shin guards."

Kathie Diapoulis, who succeeded Adele as president of WAGS, remembers that by then few doubted that she meant what she said. "All she had to do was pick up the phone, and 20,000 parents and little girls would be on your back the next day," she said in *Soccerhead*, Jim Haner's book about the rise of youth soccer.

"I was truly obnoxious," Adele allows.

Today, Adele's basement serves as headquarters of the region one U.S. Youth Soccer Association. There are pictures of Adele with various soccer greats—Pele shaking her hand as he presents her with the National Soccer Coaches Association of America award for exceptional service as female volunteer of the year for her region; Adele being honored by the NSCAA with their Youth Long-Term Achievement Award.

She is a small woman with a no-nonsense haircut and the gravelly voice that comes in part from decades of yelling on the soccer field.

"My son used to say, you know I love for you to come to my games. But if you're going to yell, you'll have to leave," she says. The same intensity that she brought to her efforts on behalf of WAGS didn't necessarily prove effective when she was coaching her daughter, Michelle.

"I'd see something like maybe she wasn't going after the ball fast enough. I'd yell at her; she'd yell at me . . . " She shakes her head. "It was so stupid. I embarrassed her, and she was a damn good player."

As a grandmother, Adele has gained perspective that surprises even her. "I see other parents doing that now, and I think, *You stupid idiot. You just did the worst thing you could do for the kid; you took him completely out of the game.*"

Now Michelle juggles roles as her daughter's coach and the WAGS tournament director. Adele lives down the block and is a regular at Devon's games. Some of Devon's favorite times take place at tournaments where being Adele's granddaughter earns her special recognition (and sometimes free balls or rides in golf carts). That is when she sees that her grandma is not special just to her. "Life would be so totally different if I didn't have her. It wouldn't be fun," she says. "When she comes to my games, it makes me feel like I want to play my best. At tournaments, it's like everyone knows her and they're like, 'You're Adele's granddaughter? Cool!' "

As the late summer sky darkens with clouds, Michelle considers her mom, who has run over to kick the ball around with Devon in their backyard. "Now I'm coaching and yelling and she's Grandma—everything the kids do is great and she's, well, she's sweet."

Adele laughs at the reversal. When she was in Michelle's position, she was hyper aware of time, whether it was that shown on the clock on the field marking the half or that slipping away from girls who were blocked from playing. She became a mother and coach who regarded time as dynamic, and she had little patience for those who were not mindful of it.

With Devon's birth came a sense that time could also be fluid, without beginning or end. Adele gets to be the grandparent who watches from the sidelines, who delights in her grandkids' triumphs, who helps them handle their defeats and revels in their successes.

"You don't really get it until you're holding your grandchild." Her eyes fill and there's a catch in her voice. "You're holding a lifeline, and you can't imagine how that makes you feel."

That lifeline wraps both arms around her grandmother and mugs for the camera; both of them stand there though rain begins to fall and Devon is in her new uniform, with its sharp emblem and matching shorts. But why worry about rain and mud? Devon knows that the uniform belongs to her.

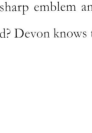

Bubbe's on the couch, Samantha at her feet, Daniel by her side.
Matthew, her oldest grandchild is 1,300 miles away

and present via cell phone. The three grandkids, are decidedly technocentric, devotees of e-mail and text messaging and phones that transmit sounds and images.

Bubbe, who lives in Northbrook, Illinois, is of the letter-writing generation. She is famous for missives that so move her grandchildren that they have learned to open them only in private. But letters don't have the immediacy of an e-mail or text-message or say, a four-way conference call, which the grandkids recently found handy.

Matthew, twenty-five, was at his job in music supervision at 20th Century Fox in Los Angeles; Samantha, twenty-two, was at her job as an account executive for Infinity Broadcasting in Chicago, and Daniel was at the University of Iowa, where he is a freshman. They had the idea to get Bubbe on the line.

"That was the funniest thing ever," Matthew says. Bubbe spent the first twenty minutes of the conversation trying to figure out where the kids were and the rest of the conversation marveling at the genius who invented the tele-conference.

For this gathering, they had hoped to top that by setting up a video conference, an idea that inspired a brief wager on Bubbe's reaction. It was not to be. A storm played havoc with the satellite transmission.

As it happened, the cell phone/speakerphone duo proved agent enough. "Are you there, Matthew?" Bubbe asks urgently of the black box

Bernice Wallis,
Daniel, Samantha
& Matthew
Libman

Enjoying the afternoon sun outside Bernice's daughter's home in suburban Illinois, (left to right): Bernice Wallis, Daniel Libman, Samantha Libman, and Matthew Libman.

on the coffee table. "Can you hear me?"

"It's taken Bubbe seven years to learn how to use her cell phone," Daniel says.

"She still doesn't know how," Samantha declares. "She told me the other day."

Bubbe repeats, "Matthew?"

"I'm here, Bubbe."

To Sam and Daniel, she says, "I don't think Matthew can hear us."

"Bubbe!" Matthew says. "I can hear you just fine."

Bubbe, a.k.a. Bernice Wallis, is an eighty-something woman who has seen more than her share of heartache. She was raised during the Depression, lost two husbands, and worked while raising two daughters, often on her own. She has lived through divorces (her daughter's), pain (cancer, severe arthritis), and, increasingly, the deaths of lifelong friends.

But she would much prefer to talk about the joy she draws from her family, her two daughters, Susan Handelman and Joie Scott and their husbands, but especially her grandchildren who, in even their ordinary efforts, make her life extraordinary.

"Everybody in our life knows about Bubbe," Samantha says. "Everybody calls her Bubbe. All my friends, and friends of friends, they're like, 'We really want to meet your mom, but we really, really want to meet Bubbe.' "

Daniel says, "Bubbe's got charisma."

"Bubbe's got *major* charisma," Matthew says

Their grandmother has loomed large in their lives from the time they were born, and they have trunkloads of Bubbe stories.

"Wait, this is the best!" Samantha says. "When I was in college, we'd sit around and in front of all my roommates, I'd play phone messages that Bubbe left. I'd shout, 'Message from Bubbe! Message from Bubbe!' And everyone would gather around and get all excited."

Bubbe herself is laughing so hard now that she is near tears. "And what was the message? I love you? I miss you?"

"She'd be like, 'Sami? Is this thing working? It's Bubbe!' "

"Yeah, yeah," says Daniel. "But she'd always have to tell you who it is, like you wouldn't know. 'Daniel? Are you there? It's Bubbe!' "

"But she wouldn't say 'It's Bubbe' until the middle of the message," Samantha says. "She'd say, 'How are you? What are you doing? Are you doing something fun?' " She pauses for effect. " 'It's Bubbe!' "

"And she'd always be worried that she's disturbing you," Daniel notes. "She'll always say, 'Sorry to bother you. I know you're busy. You don't need to call back. I just want you to know that I love you.' "

When they were kids, they had an official Bubbe day, the once-weekly day that they'd spend with their grandmother. Always, she'd arrive armed with an abundant spirit and a bag of treats. For Samantha, she'd bring lipsticks or little perfumes, whatever came with her most recent makeup purchase. "I have the world's largest collection of cosmetic bags," Samantha notes. "Even tonight when I picked her up, she said, 'Look what I have for you.' " Today, it was peanut butter cups (sans the makeup case), a food gift commonly associated with Bubbe.

Here, for the record, is an abbreviated list of Bubbe foods: chocolate-covered raisins, peanut butter cups, fresh-squeezed orange juice, ginger ale, sour candies, Pringles potato chips, chocolate-covered cherries.

Traveling with Bubbe, even to the drugstore, gave her grandchildren their first taste of fame. Samantha would count the number of people Bubbe knew, or the number who would approach her and comment on her dress or accessories or the loveliness of her looks. Bubbe's response—"I can't help it"—is now a family catchphrase.

"She tells everyone that," Daniel says.

"Everyone," Samantha agrees. "The other day, some random stranger came up to her to tell her how beautiful she looked, and she said that."

Then there are their favorite anecdotes about the stories that Bubbe tells them, or more likely, the way she tells them, generally peppered with Yiddish and nearly always with a hearty dose of hyperbole.

"When I tell a story, I definitely don't lie," says Samantha. "But I exaggerate like nobody else. I'll say, 'Oh, it was the best thing ever.' Or 'It was the greatest night of my life.' All because of Bubbe. She calls me every week, and she'll be like, 'You've got to go see that picture. It was the best movie I've ever seen.'"

"It's true," attests Matthew. "All of us talk with a gratuitous use of superlatives, always."

"But here's something people don't know about Bubbe," Daniel says. "Bubbe is unfailingly polite, and her exterior is every bit the lady."

"I *am* a lady," Bubbe confirms.

"But privately," Daniel continues, Bubbe loves dirty jokes. "She loves to hear them. She loves to tell them. She loves everything about them."

Bubbe is hysterical. "You can't put *that* in the book."

"Everything we'll say, she'll tell you that you can't put it in the book," Samantha confides. A regular feature of Samantha's twice-weekly visits to her Bubbe is a *Sex and the City* viewing and discussion. On Wednesday-night visits, this is preceded by Turkey Night at the condominium club where Bubbe lives.

"The first time I went, I was dying because they were all trying to fix me up with their nephews. And then at the end, they all pulled out their cell phones and are like, 'How do you work these things?' and I'm going around the table trying to help them with their cell phones."

"But I think on a more serious note, one of Bubbe's roles is that she's the moral barometer of the family," Matthew says. "Kind of like, people will say, 'What would Jesus do?' for us it's 'What would Bubbe do?' She's been through it all and seen it all, twice."

Throughout their lives, "Do it for Bubbe" became a tool of unparalleled effectiveness, which their mother, Susan, found useful to compel behavior when other methods failed.

"Whatever it was, Mom would always say, 'Do it for your Bubbe,'" Daniel deadpans. "Like, 'Mop the floor.' 'I just mopped the floor.' 'Do it for your Bubbe.'"

"People always say to Mom, how did you do it on your own?" Samantha says (their parents divorced when Daniel was a baby; Samantha and Matthew were in elementary school). Matthew says, "Well, a lot of it is the role models we had. When we do something, we want to do it the best we can for Bubbe. Not because we're afraid of being reprimanded, but because we know how much joy it would bring her."

"But I also think it allowed us to take risks and try different things," Daniel notes. "You didn't want to disappoint. But you also did it because you had that support and you knew how much she wanted to brag."

Bubbe kept a book of accomplishments and important moments for each child in a particular year. On their birthdays and at other milestones, she'd write letters filled with details about the events of that year, always adding a reminder that nothing mattered more than family.

Collectively, the letters tell of the grandchildren's transformation, their evolution from small children (with big accomplishments) to adolescents (bigger accomplishments) then to adults (greatness on the horizon):

Dear Daniel: Now that you are five years old, you are no longer a baby, but you will always be the youngest in the family. . . . I don't know how it is possible, but each year you get more beautiful.

The year started with our cruise celebrating Papa's 75th birthday. We had so much fun. When we were getting aboard, you looked up and said, "Holy Ships!" . . . You met the captain and saluted him.

This was the year for Batman, Dick Tracy, *and* Ninja Turtles. *You played basketball in the backyard with Sami and Matthew and his friends. You learned how to add 1 + 1, 2+2 and so on. And you made your first commercial. You still love matzo balls and chicken soup, pizza, chicken nuggets, and toasted cheese. . . . You are a lovable, wonderful boy, who everybody loves, and Papa and I are very proud of you.*

Dear Matthew, begins one written in honor of his fourteenth birthday, which included a picture of Matthew as a baby with a guitar: *The enclosed picture should be saved for posterity. If you don't know what that word means, this would be a good time to pull out your dictionary. I guess you were serious about the guitar at an early age. When you become a STAR you can use it for publicity. . . .*

Remember I told you, if you reach for the stars you can get to the moon. . . .

And then, in honor of his twenty-first birthday: *Matthew, dear, I am so grateful and lucky to be alive to celebrate your twenty-first birthday. It seems like yesterday that I went to Sabbath services to pray and give thanks the morning that you were born. . . . A grandmother may give love, but I thank you for the love and respect you have returned to me. Your mom gave you life and perhaps I have helped sustain your life in a small way. . . . You have a God-given gift of a great musical talent and many miles to go to reach fulfillment. . . . I hope that I may have the "nachas" [pleasure] of knowing that I believed in and am so proud of my special grandson*

Reflecting on the letters, Matthew says, "We learned fairly quickly that you didn't want to open them in public."

"They make you cry hysterically," says Sam.

My dear Samantha: How could you be eighteen years old so soon? . . . I am so fortunate to be able to share the years of pleasure that you have given me. Beauty is as beauty does and I am so proud of you. I tell everybody that the wrinkles in my face are smiling lines from the joy I have from my grandchildren. . . . I "kvell" [burst with joy] from your honesty, your determination, your ambition, and the love and respect you show your family and friends. . . . May your life be as beautiful as you are.

Thinking about them, Samantha talks of friends who don't have a Bubbe, a thought that brings tears to her eyes. "What's wrong, Bubala?" Bernice asks her. "Oh, Matthew. Samantha is crying. I've made her cry."

"No, no, Bubbe," Samantha assures her. "This is happy crying." She's about to explain this, but she is distracted by a muffled beep, a message on her cell phone. A friend has sent a text message. It reads: "How's Bubbe?"

When Estella Wheeler learned she was going to be a grandmother, she did not feel the usual swell of delight.

What she felt instead was something closer to fear.

Estella owns a hat shop in northeast Washington, D.C., which is itself a full-time job. Her husband Leroy had just been in a car accident and needed care. Her vision of being a grandmother was shaped in part by her own mother, who took care of Estella's kids only in emergencies when Estella was sick, for instance. But Estella knew that in this case, becoming a grandmother would be different.

"It's like starting over again for some of us. I would be the sole supporter of those grandchildren; I knew that's how it was going to be," Estella says. "I'm thinking, how on earth am I going to take care of those grandchildren?"

She is surrounded by women from the Faith Temple Church, a circle of grandmothers who punctuate Estella's thoughts with "that's right" and "amen." Together, they are the equivalent of an executive network, providing each other with support both concrete and ephemeral, with baby seats and advice, all of it wrapped in their shared faith.

Nearly all of these women grew up in rural North Carolina. If they didn't know one other directly, they knew about one another, as was common in small southern communities of the 1940s and 1950s. They grew up with grandmothers who regularly raised children, who took over for friends, daughters, and nieces who headed north to build better lives. One by one, often unbeknownst to one another, the women left their tightly knit community and made their way to Maryland and Washington, D.C. They married or worked, had children, and often fell out of touch.

Estella Wheeler

At their church in Washington, D.C., (front row, left to right): Estella Wheeler, Priscilla Langston, Dorothy Sue Langston; (middle row, left to right): Josie Mae Millard, Ruby Joyner; (back row, left to right): Nancy Suggs Shivers, Doris Finch.

Years later, on an anonymous street, inside the walls of a simple church, they found one another again. Now in a new community, where children often grow up without two-parent families, safe places to play, or great schools, these grandmothers offer up a first and last line of defense, a safety net built of prayer, experience, and determination.

"Working together and holding each other up is the only way to survive in this world," says Dorothy "Dot" Langston. The women, all in their Sunday best, are gathered around table to talk about the role grandmothers play in their community. "I hold up my corner. She holds up her corner, and someone else grabs that corner over there. We build these children up together. We hold these children up so they can go forth and be whatever they want to be."

When Estella learned she was going to be a grandmother, she turned to Nancy Shivers. "I said, 'Nancy, I'm not ready for this. What am I going to do?' You talk about a shoulder to lean on—I don't know how *she* kept upright. I was constantly, constantly leaning on her."

There were sheer physical demands on Estella's time and space, as well as on her pocketbook, which was already supporting her husband and one grandchild who, at the time, was three. One of the women brought Estella a crib. Another brought a changing table. Together, they worked to rearrange Estella's house to make room where it seemed there was none. They organized a grandbaby shower.

"That's what you do in a circle like this," says Dot's daughter, Priscilla, who at age forty-three is the youngest grandmother of the group. "Each of us alone does not have everything, but together we give each other all we need."

"This woman here," Dot nods to Sue Langston, who has eleven grandchildren, "I would go to see her, just to talk, and she got me through. She'd say, 'You can't change what's going to happen. Sometimes God acts in ways we don't understand. But you can come here, come to me. Tell me what you need.' "

At the time, Dot needed babysitting help, and so the women offered up either themselves or others they knew who could help. They are strengthened, they say, by the profound role that faith plays in their lives. But they are also drawing on a legacy of the lessons they observed when they were children.

Each one of them offers up a story from her childhood—of a sister, a friend, an aunt who left home to find work or build a better life and left behind children for the grandmother to raise.

"Many times, all they could do was leave them with the grandparents," Priscilla says. "They didn't have a choice. They didn't leave their children because they wanted to. They left because they wanted to create a better life for those children. My mother didn't leave me because she wanted to. But my grandmother was there with a lot of wisdom. When grandmothers and mothers join together to raise the children, you're going to turn out better children. Whatever the mother is lacking, the grandmother has to give. For my children, what I could not give them as a young mother, they were able to get from their grandmother. Children can't help but be better for it."

But the women emphasize that raising children in the 21st century in Washington, D.C., is far different from the world they knew as children.

"I don't think people know the total responsibility that we take in our grandchildren's lives," Estella says emphatically. "A grandmother used to spoil the kids and send them home. Or if she was raising them, there was someone to share the responsibility, the mother or an aunt. For this generation, responsibility has a totally different meaning."

Instead of spoiling their grandchildren, these women often find themselves in the role of disciplining them, setting limits where the parents can't or won't. Even well-meaning parents may not do enough.

"One thing I see a lot of these days is that mothers want to be friends with their children; they want to be on the same level," Dot says, in part to her daughter, Priscilla, who smiles in recognition. "That's where grandparents have to step in. I tell my grandkids, 'You can be open with me, and I'll be as open with you as I can be. But you are not on my level.

You can't speak to me as if you're talking to a friend. There's got to be respect.'"

"If the grandmothers weren't there, I don't think many of these kids would make it," Sue says. "In my case, their mothers are working or going to school and I'm happy to help. I better be, because I've got so many grandchildren!"

"There are so many children you hear about who have lost their mothers, or their grandmothers don't take them and they end up in the foster care system and then they are lost."

"That's one thing about the older generation, at least where we came from in the South," notes Ruby Joyner. "A grandparent would never, *never* turn away a baby." Ruby remembers her own mother traveling north to pick up a nephew whom she brought back and raised as her own son—as Ruby's brother.

These grandmothers see a generation at risk of losing that heritage. They fear that their children and grandchildren will turn away from the church, which is central to all of their lives. "You want to know the truth," Priscilla says. "My greatest fear of losing these women, of losing this generation, is that I don't want to be one of the last remaining grandmothers standing alone praying for our grandchildren. After all the prayers that our grandparents said for us, and their ancestors said for them, if we lose that connection, then the future generation will be lost."

Dorothy Langston nods. "Sometimes, you're going through these horrible things, things that are just devastating, and you think you're alone. And then you talk to these ladies and you realize that, as a grandmother, you are never alone."

"Bella, Bella, Bella!" Olympia Dukakis spots her granddaughter, Isabella, and can't wait to get her arms around her.

This is a rare moment in Dukakis's New York apartment, when Olympia is not on a set or in a theater; when her husband, the actor Louis Zorich (who is performing nearby), can swing home for an hour; when all the grand-children are coming by: Isabella, Sofia, and the new baby, Luka.

They are all together, and a photographer will be on hand. What better time to get a group portrait of the grandparents and their progeny? It's August, but what Olympia has in mind is a shot that might work for the family Christmas card, an image that captures the joy of grandparenthood: Olympia, Louis, and three happy little ones.

Isabella buries herself in her grandmother's arms and then twirls on command, a picture-ready six-year-old with lush, dark hair and an obedi-ent oldest-child nature. Next comes Sofia, who has just turned three.

She bounces into the apartment but stands back for a moment, then dutifully offers a hug before running off. In Sofia, Olympia sees herself as a child, full of spunk and will, a fighter who knows how to pick herself up after a fall. "It's her way or the highway," Olympia laughs.

They are all there, the grandkids and Olympia and Louis, who abandons himself to the pleasure of the moment. They gather on a couch for a pose. Sunlight streams in through the floor-to-ceiling window, illuminating their faces and falling on the girls' shoulders in a halo of light. But just as Olympia is about to say, "Smile, everyone!" Sofia decides she's had enough.

Olympia Dukakis, Isabella, Sofia & Luka Zorich

Playing in Olympia's Manhattan apartment (left to right): Isabella Zorich, Olympia Dukakis, Luka Zorich, and Sofia Zorich.

She stands up in protest and unleashes a loud, defiant scream, which startles baby Luka, who begins to cry, which sends Isabella into a whirlwind effort to coax her sister into compliance. What was to be a cinematic moment becomes the mess that is real life.

Olympia throws her head back in delight and shouts, "Get the shot! Get the shot!"

This may not be the image most families have in mind, but then Olympia knows that Sofia's outburst is, in its own way, a loving tribute to her grandmother, who for so much of her life fought for the right to be heard.

"I used to do exactly what Sofia did—scream and cry and fight," Olympia laughs. "Now, that's not always a good thing. But being a fighter gets you places and I learned that from my mother, to fight for myself."

That same spirit has fed Olympia's legendary career as an actress in film, theater, and television and has helped her create memorable characters: Rose Castorini in *Moonstruck*, the role that earned her an Academy Award; Clairee in *Steel Magnolias;* others in dozens of theatrical productions and films where she has brought depth and power to portrayals of even the most marginalized characters.

Her voice alone has a signature all its own. But as a child, she was discouraged from using it. Her parents instilled in their first generation of Greek Americans a fierce work ethic and a devotion to their heritage and the values that shape it. Growing up in Lowell, Massachusetts, Olympia felt stifled by her mother, who tried desperately to raise her daughter according to the standards of traditional Greek life, where girls were to be seen but rarely heard. That struggle would last a lifetime.

"I was the poster child for the bad Greek daughter," Olympia says.

One vivid memory of Olympia's childhood is seeing her mother so enraged that she would grab her neck as if she were being strangled and fall to the floor, writhing in silence, unable to express her anger. Years later, when Olympia was traveling among Greek villages where her grandparents were raised, she realized that the display of withheld rage was the only way women in some villages there had to express themselves.

But at the time, her mother's performance infuriated young Olympia and fed her determination to declare an identity of her own making.

"There's a lot of pressure from the outside world, telling you to be like everyone else, don't rock the boat, take the easy way out," she wrote in her autobiography. "When you fight that, you naturally put yourself on the outside, and I spent a lot of my life feeling like an outsider. When I was younger, I took this as an indictment, but I grew to understand it was not just the road I'd carved out for myself through sheer stubbornness, it was the only road I wanted to take."

Olympia found comfort in her paternal grandmother, or Yia Yia, who helped raise her. She was a warm, soft-spoken woman who delighted in Olympia's antics in a way her mother never could. When she died, Olympia was twelve and was not allowed to see her, a fact that still haunts her. "She was very, very affectionate, and I just loved her so much," she says. "She's always with me. I feel her, still."

Olympia was tough and athletic but inherited from her mother a flair for the dramatic. She found her way to Boston University's Master of

Fine Arts program. There she discovered the theater and for the first time felt that she knew who she was to be. By 1988, when she was nominated for an Academy Award, she was a seasoned actress with dozens of credits to her name. She had raised three children, worked around the clock on screen, stage, and television, and faced a terrifying time when her husband Louis was severely injured in an automobile accident. She had battled decades of bias that said that she could only play "ethnic" parts, or that as a woman, she couldn't convey the motivations of a man.

Hearing her name announced as the winner of the Academy Award that night, she felt herself "floating on a current of ancestral energy—the energy that had blessed and cursed me for five decades."

In the same way that she fought typecasting as an actress or mother, she resists stereotypes that define what a grandmother is supposed to be. Rather, she brings to her relationship with her grandchildren all the complexity and experience that comes from a woman who has lived for seventy-three years and is still finding out who she is.

"The relationship is certainly idealized. I've heard people say that their whole life changes, that they're so much in love, but it's not like that for me," she says. "My work is very real for me, very much the focus. I travel and hustle, and so my grandkids are not the focus.

We want to think that as we get older, things get simpler, we have more happiness, more wisdom; we want to think that. That's not necessarily true. I think things can get very complicated, very scary because of aging, illness, loss of friends and family. There are some very difficult issues that people deal with as they get older. We tend not to be able to tell those stories too well in our society."

Now that she is Yia Yia to Isabella, Sofia, and Luka, she wonders about their lives, the experiences they'll have that she won't see. It is one reason that in 2003, Olympia wrote *Ask Me Again Tomorrow*, a critically acclaimed look at the transformations that shaped her life. The book is dedicated to her children and grandchildren. "I want them to know where they came from," she says.

"You know, there is something so sweet and wonderful about children, and to be around them, it just makes me so, so happy," she says. "They are just so tender, so dear, and you know as a mother you have it with your own children, but you have so much worry with your children. Now, it makes me happy just to watch them."

Being a grandmother for Olympia is not a role but an evolution, a continuation from the lessons of motherhood. "It makes me very aware that I spent a good deal more time worrying and hustling than I wish I had," she says. "I wish I had more time to be frivolous with my kids, to do mindless tasks like blowing bubbles."

Just then, Isabella pokes her head into the room where Olympia is sitting, showing her something she's drawn. The cameras have been put away. Louis is back at the theater, Luka is sleeping, and the house is quiet. Olympia sees Sofia near the couch where she has opened a gift that Olympia bought for her, an elephant that blows bubbles. Olympia, barefoot, sits on the floor next to her granddaughter and joins in.

Kristie was at her grandmother's house.
Kelley was at summer camp.

Neither of these facts felt significant except in retrospect, when Ruth Slagle searched for a sign, something that might have told her what was to come.

Kristie was distracted. Ruth remembers that, remembers thinking that something was wrong. She prodded until finally Kristie said, "Oh, Grandma. Mom is so unhappy."

By the end of that day, Kristie and Kelley's mother, Shelly, would be dead, a suicide. Ruth would have the awful task of telling Kristie first and then driving to Kelley's camp to tell her. In the weeks and months that followed, Kristie and Kelley would lose every constant in their lives. They would leave their home, their friends, and their school. They would move in with their father, his new wife, and her kids—an uneasy alliance at best. Already, only teenagers, they seemed destined for a life defined by loss.

"You know," Kelley says, "my friends say all the time, 'Man, Kelley, your life must have been so painful and bizarre.' I always say, 'It was.' But the one thing I always had in my life was my grandmother. We've had so much loss, but we've had so much love."

Kristie nods. "She was—always has been—our rock. It's strange to realize that one relationship can transform your life."

Ruth Slagle is a thin, precise woman with a dignified manner. She is the kind of woman who, in a different era, would herd the cows, sow the land, cook the food, and entertain with grace. She shares with her granddaughters a singular history, a relationship that transformed tragedy into strength and love.

Ruth Slagle, Kristie Slagle Kienstra & Kelley Slagle

Kristie Slagle Kienstra, Ruth Slagle, and Kelley Slagle in a park in Kansas City, Missouri.

"What would have happened if you weren't there, Grandma?" Kristie asks. "We wouldn't have had an education, we wouldn't have had the love, we wouldn't have been who we are."

"Well," Ruth harrumphs, "that wasn't going to happen."

Shelly was the daughter Ruth never had. She was only sixteen when she began dating Ruth's son, Bill. Ruth remembers that when she first met her, she couldn't stop looking at Shelly. She was struck by her beauty (she was a model) but also her sweetness, a vulnerability that made Ruth want to protect her.

Even before the marriage, Ruth became a mother to Shelly, arranging her travels to college, helping with her room, and eventually assisting with her wedding. By the time Kelley and then Kristie were born, it seemed natural that the girls would spend as much time with their grandmother as they did at their own home.

"My friends would see the girls with me all the time, and they would say, 'Shelly just dumps those girls on you.' And I'd tell them, 'Oh, no, she does not. I love every minute of it.' "

If there were signs of depression, Ruth and the girls never saw them. Shelly created a home filled with inventiveness and whimsy, elaborate birthday parties, outings that felt like grand adventures. Always it was the four of them: Shelly, Kelley, Kristie, and Ruth.

Their grandmother's house was the place they went when their mother was working, when they wanted to run away, when they wanted a place where they knew they could do anything and still be loved. "We loved our mother more than anything," said Kelley. "But there was always something special about going to Grandma's, something about that relationship that, even as a kid, you realize from the get-go this is the place you want to be."

"Grandparents don't say no," Ruth offers.

"Yeah, well, there's that," Kelley says. "And I have to say, I was a terror. A very rotten child."

"You were mischievous and determined," Ruth corrects her.

Together, Ruth and Shelly took the girls everywhere—to town, to the theater, to restaurants. What they could not afford, Shelly would create. She was inventive even in discipline: when the girls fought, she sat them nose-to-nose and insisted they not laugh. "I learned so much about parenting from her," Ruth says. "We have wonderful, wonderful memories, and she gave these girls a foundation that is so very special. And I will always be grateful to her for sharing these girls with me."

When Shelly told Ruth that she and Bill were getting a divorce, Ruth was devastated. Shelly's second marriage was a difficult one; her new husband, Steve, tried to keep Ruth out of their lives. Shelly arranged clandestine meetings, assuring Ruth that nothing would divide them.

Then, one week in June, when Kelley was at camp, Shelly called Ruth to ask if Kristie could visit for the weekend. It was Shelly's high school reunion.

Ruth was delighted. "You know she can," she remembers telling her. Even when Kristie was young, she bore striking similarities to her grandmother: a quiet watchfulness, a traditional taste in clothes, and the sensitivity that told Kristie that her mother was in trouble; that something was terribly wrong. Though she ordinarily jumped at the chance to visit her grandmother, Kristie was reluctant to leave and begged one of her mother's friends to stay with Shelly.

When Kristie arrived at her grandmother's, Ruth saw her distress. "Oh, Grandma," Kristie finally told her. "Steve is making Mom miserable."

Ruth told Kristie what she believed: The pending divorce was wearing on all of them; once it was finalized, their lives would return to normal.

"You know, the day I learned their mother and my son were divorcing was one of the worst days of my life—a horrible day. But then, when I learned about Shelly's death, I thought I just couldn't live through it."

Kelley remembers that moment at camp when she looked up to see her grandparents' car. Her first thought—that they were there to surprise her—gave way to the certainty that something awful had happened.

The girls were sent to their father. They knew that they could live with their grandparents, but Kelley feared that she was too much for them. "I was very angry," she says. "I really acted up."

Their father lived in Paola, Kansas, forty minutes away. He was in a new marriage of his own, with a woman who had her own children. Kelley and Kristie sensed that she felt threatened by them. The girls were relegated to the basement of a very small house and were not to touch the other children's things. Even food was labeled so they'd know what was theirs.

"I never knew much of this," Ruth says. The girls knew that their father enlarged the basement, made a separate entrance for them, decorated their rooms. What they did not know was that their grandparents provided the money and incentive to ensure that the girls had a place that felt like a home.

Ruth and her husband surprised the girls with trips. Through them, Kristie and Kelley would see the world. Birthdays were celebrations for both of them, with birthday and "unbirthday" gifts. And when it came time for Kelley to apply for college, Ruth and her husband hovered over her applications, ensuring they were in the mail before the deadline, visiting universities so Kelley would know that every opportunity was hers to take.

The three of them are gathered in Kelley's home in Kansas City, where Kelley and Ruth still live. Kristie has moved to Florida with her husband. At eighty-seven, Ruth lives on her own, travels extensively, cares for her often-younger friends, and tries to rein in her granddaughters' anxieties about her welfare.

"They are so good to me, both of them," Ruth says. "They are considerate, loving . . ."

"Bossy," Kelley adds.

"Bossy," Ruth agrees.

"When I reflect on my life," Kelley says, "it's not the sadness that comes out. I've been given gifts—a life so blessed. . . ."

"But you had that wonderful background with your mother," Ruth insists.

Ruth looks down at her hands, then at the girls. "Her relationship with those girls—they just had such a happy life."

Kelley crosses the living room to retrieve a picture of her mother. She passes it to Kristie, who passes it to Ruth. In the frame is a picture of a smiling woman with the hair, the eyes, the upturned mouth that is in the

face of Kristie and Kelley. "I think if it hadn't been for Grandma, the family would have been broken, everything would have broken," Kelley says. Most of their friends never met their mother, and may not know their father. But they all know Ruth.

"Every single person who meets her says, 'Oh, I want to be just like your grandmother,'" Kristie insists.

"Oh dear," Ruth says.

"It's true, Grandma. I go to visit my friends' grandparents and their houses are dark and they're depressing and . . ."

"Well, honey, they might be sick."

"No, no," Kristie says laughing. "They just—she's just so hip."

Ruth rolls her eyes. "Oh, boy."

"I'll call her all the time," Kelley says, "like, when I'm having a dinner party, I'll call and say, 'What should I serve with this?' She just knows those things. Or with relationships. She tells me to kill them with kindness, or to step back and look at another person's point of view."

"Oh, my," laughs Ruth. "I have them snowed but good."

The truth is that Ruth remains intimately involved in the details of the girls' lives. Kristie sees a lot of herself in Ruth. Kristie calls every day from Florida, sometimes three times a day.

"You're the spark plug," Ruth kids Kelley.

"She never takes me seriously," Kelley grumbles. "Today, she told me that my haircut was horrible—that I never get a good haircut. She wouldn't dare say that to Kristie, because Kristie would be worried about her hair for the rest of her life."

"Well you keep Grandma's life exciting," Kristie tells her sister.

Last year, for the first time since Ruth lost her husband, she went on a trip with the girls to Europe. They toured the Christmas markets on the Danube, went to Austria and Turkey. The trip was for people over the age of fifty-five, but an exception was made for Kristie, Kelley, and their cousin, Jenny.

"It was wonderful," Ruth exclaims. "A perfect, perfect trip."

"We had a blast," Kelley says. "We still keep in contact with two or three couples we met."

Ruth refuses to get e-mail or a cell phone, so sometimes she'll come home after being out for a few hours to find five increasingly desperate messages from the girls.

"I want to connect. I want to know that she's doing OK," Kristie says. "I keep telling her I wish she would move down to Florida, but I know that's not going to happen because she has a very vibrant social life."

In part because of her grandmother, Kelley works with the elderly. "I see aging as such an honor, and I see people who are so wonderful to be around, so enriching. I'm shocked by how few people feel that way."

But they know the painful side of their age differences all too well. "It's just so hard when you're so close to someone and there's such an age difference. I keep telling her I want to go with her."

Both girls are silent for a moment. "The other night, I had this dream that she died," Kristie says later. "And it was like in this dream, it wasn't horrible, but natural. But when I woke up, I thought, *Oh, my God. There's so much I should have done.*"

Ruth sighs. "Kristie, you have to let loose. I can't live forever."

"OK," Kristie says, forcing a slight smile. "Just live to 120."

The rows of cotton stretched impossibly long. Lillie Owens was twelve, but she already knew not to look too far ahead.

Lillie Owens, Kendall & Mitchell Elie

Lillie Owens, Kendall Elie, and Mitchell Elie throwing rocks into Lake Michigan.

Better to keep her eyes down; if she looked beyond what was at hand, she'd lose heart.

Lillie lived in Morganza, Louisiana, in a shotgun home that had no electricity, no plumbing, and no running water. In wintertime, she went to school. But springtime brought picking season, and Lillie would leave school to work the cotton fields with her mother. It was dull, sometimes painful work, and to pass the time, Lillie told her mother stories, fantasies about the life she was going to live.

She would live in a big city with so many lights that night would always look like day, she said. She would have a car and a fine, big house, and she'd go to the movies whenever she wanted.

Her mother would laugh and shake her head. "Lillie, you are a dreamer," she'd say. But then she'd ask Lillie to tell her more, and Lillie would use words to draw a picture of the life she was certain she'd have. "You know," her mother told her, "if you dream long enough, that just might happen. Dreams do come true."

Now seventy, Lillie Owens is a tall, strong woman who insists that she is not good with words. She is not given to writing like her daughter, Tannette Johnson-Elie—or Tina, as her mother calls her—a newspaper columnist at the *Milwaukee Journal Sentinel*. She does not have the educational opportunities of her grandsons, Kendall and Mitchell, twelve and eight, who she insists have a better grasp of grammar than she does.

"I always was a dreamer and still am, in a sense," Lillie says. "But see, when you're in that hot sun, you don't look up and say, 'Oh God, I'm not at the end.'

You just keep picking and telling stories, and that was the only way to get from row to row."

It is a method that Lillie followed until, one day, she saw that her grandchildren were inhabiting the world that she'd imagined.

A black girl's prospects for employment in the Louisiana of the 1940s were confined to the cotton fields or a white family's home, where she could work as a "domestic." When she was twelve, Lillie left the cotton fields to work for Jane Vosburg, a woman with two little girls and a husband who was often traveling on business. Inside the Vosburg home, Lillie was treated warmly. "Miss Jane took a liking to me, I think because I took so much time and care with her girls and she knew I would do anything for them," Lillie says.

"We did everything together and she made me feel so comfortable," Lillie says. "There was a lot of prejudice but I was not subjected to it." Lillie worked there for five years, until, at age seventeen, she met James Owens. He was a kind, hard-working man who planned to move North to work construction. Miss Jane sought out Lillie's mother to make sure that James was a good man for Lillie to marry. "She said, 'I wouldn't want Lil to be hurt by anyone,'" Lillie recalls. "I thought that was so incredible, that she cared for me that much. I never forgot that."

The young newlyweds moved to Chicago, where James had a construction job and moved into a home they imagined would be filled with children. Lillie began work for the U.S. Postal Service. She had one miscarriage and then another before doctors told her that she could not have a baby. It was one of the lowest points of her life.

"I saw myself with a child," she said. "It's what you think you're going to do."

Ironically, Lillie's sixteen-year-old brother, Sam, had just gotten a woman pregnant. The woman was at least twenty years older than he was, and he intended to marry her. But to do so, Sam needed his mother's written permission, which she refused to give.

After giving birth, the woman drove to Sam's house and said that she could not care for the child. "My mother called me right then," Lillie remembers. "She said, 'Lil, I've got you the most beautiful baby in the world.'"

That weekend, Lillie and James drove to Louisiana. They approached the mother, who signed the baby over to them. On the long drive home to Chicago, Lillie and James said her name over and over, as if to make their "Tina" real.

Lillie and James raised Tannette in Hyde Park, a community south of Chicago then known for its diversity and tolerance. Built around the University of Chicago and its institutions, it fostered in Tannette her own dreams to accomplish things her mother never could.

When Tannette was admitted to Bradley University in Peoria, Illinois, Lillie and James were hard-pressed to pay for the private college. But they never questioned the wisdom of sending their daughter there.

"Here's this woman who grew up in abject poverty, and there is no end to the sacrifices she has made for me," Tannette says. "And yet all you would ever see is the love that she gives."

Lillie Owens lives in a red brick home on a street of red brick homes

in a Chicago neighborhood that does not call attention to itself. Hers is a modest house with a small, gracious dining room, where Lillie has set out china cups for coffee and a plate of cookies. It's not like the home in Gurnee where Tannette and her husband, Jean, now live with their boys—the first time Lillie looked up into its cathedral ceilings and expansive rooms, she nearly lost her balance. "Tina, this is a mansion," she had said. "Ma," Tannette replied. "This is not a mansion."

But it's clear the home of Lillie's dreams is the one where she now lives, filled, as she'd once hoped, with children. It's her grandsons who have the run of it now, racing up and down stairs, playing the video games Lillie has installed for them. Since 1996, the year her husband died and Lillie retired from the Postal Service, she's spent half her week helping to care for the boys.

"They are my miracles," she says. "First Tina, and now I have these two."

On a bright Sunday, Lillie and her grandsons wander along the edge of South Shore beach. Each boy takes an arm. Kendall, as the oldest, proclaims that he'll be his grandmother's cane. This is their joke.

Their grandmother is not exactly a bystander in their escapades. She has taught them to bowl, keeps up with them on bikes, indulges their requests for fast food and baseball games. And when they find themselves too taken with their toys or new sneakers or a video game, Lillie reminds them of her life.

Tannette, watching her mother with the boys, says, "I think she will always be their teacher."

Lillie doesn't see herself that way. She just wants to tell them a story.

Several years ago, Trudy Taylor happened upon a group of girls at Alley's General Store, the local grocery near her home in Martha's Vineyard. She did not know the girls by name, nor did she know that they went to school with her granddaughter Alexandra.

"Tell me something." She gave the girls a steady, determined look. "What are the schools teaching you about sex education?" Trudy believed that she had a responsibility—if not an obligation—to speak directly and plainly about a subject that other adults tend to avoid.

The girls listened politely, then bowed out of the conversation and the store more than a little startled. But upon hearing the story, Alexandra was hardly surprised. The Trudy Taylor whom her friends met that day was the same grandmother Alexandra had come to know. "She is this enormously confident, honest person, and if she has a concern about something—whether it's me or my brother or the people on this island—she's going to tell it like it is," says Alexandra, who is now twenty-nine.

To Vineyard regulars, Trudy is an enigmatic force behind an impassioned legacy. She is the mother of legendary singer/songwriter James Taylor and his four siblings (Alex, Livingston, Kate, and Hugh, each a prominent musician and artist). At eighty-something, Trudy lives in the town of Chilmark on a remote strip of land between the small tidal inlet of Quitsa and Stonewall Pond.

Trudy's vision is rooted in this landscape, in a place that is at once harsh and beautiful. It inspires her art—her painting, cooking, knitting, gardening,

Gertrude Taylor

Trudy Taylor sitting near her garden in Chilmark, Martha's Vineyard.

writing—accomplishments so extensive that granddaughter Aretha Witham exclaims, "She's good at everything! I can't get over it." The landscape also radiates the fierce opinions and self-sufficiency that has long inspired and startled her friends, her children, and her ten grandchildren.

"I believe strongly in giving space to children to allow them to become themselves," Trudy says. "I really, really, really wanted that for my children. But there's a risk to that."

As her children rose to artistic heights, Trudy knew extremes of happiness and despair. Alex, the oldest son, died in 1993 of a heart attack related to his long struggle with alcoholism; James's and Livingston's battles with addiction stretch back to their earliest songwriting days; both James and daughter Katie fought incapacitating depressions before they were twenty years old. And yet those years only confirmed her view that children and grandchildren must be allowed to fall and fail.

"Children don't really belong to you," Trudy says. "I think you can run into trouble when you start trying to own your children. And when they are adolescents, of course, they really do break away. They have to get their own identity, but they come back again when they have put the puzzle together."

From the time Trudy was a young mother, the home on the Vineyard served as an inspiring escape. She and her husband, Isaac Taylor, were raising their children in Chapel Hill, where Isaac was a physician at the University of North Carolina.

Trudy, a native of Boston, felt isolated in the South of the 1950s. In 1969, she divorced her husband and moved the family to the Vineyard, where she winterized their simple summer house. But even before the move, good memories began to accumulate, most notably of impromptu family sing-a-longs. James played cello, Alex played violin, Kate had her dulcimer, and there was an old upright piano. The family sang everything—folk songs, hymns, Broadway tunes, radio jingles. Kitchen utensils doubled for instruments.

She signed her children up for music lessons and created a home that fostered creativity. "Often, if you ask someone who is very successful at something, 'When did you know you could do that?' the person will say, 'I knew when I was eight or nine,'" Trudy points out. "They already know where their strengths are, and your job is to be in support of that, not to try and make them into something that they know they are not. There's quite a trick to that, because so many parents think they can mold a child into what they want it to be. I don't think that's possible.

"What surprised me most about my children is that I knew they were musical, but I didn't realize what fine performers they were. Of course, you can never predict someone like a James—you can't teach that."

"She's very perceptive of individual characteristics," Isaac Taylor, Hugh's son, notes. "I think even when we were children she could recognize the ways we were receptive and create an environment that would foster our creativity."

For each grandchild, Trudy created a special book, a collection of photographs, drawings, and writings. In a family of outsized personas, the books gave each child a sense of identity, a place in the whole. "It would give me this sense of cohesion to all my family members, but it would also show me as an individual," Isaac says. "It gave me a very early sense of my connection to family and my place in it."

For each grandchild, Trudy created a special book,
a collection of photographs, drawings, and writings.
In a family of outsized personas,
the books gave each child a sense of identity.

As she aged and her children began having children of their own, Trudy expanded the limits of her own life, traveling often, sailing the Atlantic on her own, exploring talents that she hadn't yet tapped. "I just don't seem to have the fear that most people do," she says.

Aretha watched her grandmother learn to watercolor when in her seventies and become a master, a lesson that inspires Aretha in her singing and songwriting at the Berklee College of Music in Boston. "It reminds me that there is not time to stop improving yourself," she says.

Trudy sees the Chilmark home as a place that fosters self-sufficiency and the importance of family. "We make a point of getting all the generations together if a child has a birthday party or for a holiday," she says. "I think that's very important. It is a connectedness, a very good feeling, to have aunts and uncles and grandparents telling stories and playing music and delighting in each other. Parents don't always have time to provide that.

"As a grandparent, you can offer a different kind of love. You've learned so much by having children, and there's a special love that comes with the separation of a generation."

But Trudy worries that the separation that can teach children so much about life and their place in it is being tested by the geographic distance that increasingly separates children from their grandparents.

"The grandmother has the genetic component, of course. But she also holds the mythology of the family, the history, the stories that carry a family forward. What does it mean when a generation comes of age without that?"

In 2002, on Trudy's 80th birthday, her children arranged a grand celebration at the Outermost Inn, an island landmark owned and run by son Hugh and his family. Isaac, who does landscaping on the island, mowed the inn's lawn into the shape of a T. Inside, Trudy was dressed in overalls and surrounded by children, grandchildren, and close friends, who took turns singing and paying homage to her.

"Trudy's life, her spirit and energy, is that of two people," son James said in his toast. "I think mothers like their kids to be settled and happy and safe. And Trudy has the ability to be able to feel otherwise."

For her grandchildren, Trudy is a reminder that the human spirit does not rest. "When you have the ability to touch and move people, you kind of have to do it," says Aretha. "It's the same with James and Liv. They never stop. And neither does Trudy,"

Along the base of the Sangre de Cristo mountains, just east of the Tooth of Time,

New Mexico's Highway 58 banks downward to meet a gravel road. There, just beyond a sign that says CS Cattle Co., Linda Davis is waiting, ramrod straight from the tip of her boots to the top of her hat.

She nods for you to follow to the main house, where the mountains give way to vast stretches of prairie grass, and where for the past fifty years Linda has worked 250,000 acres of land, turning it into one of the largest family-owned ranching operations in New Mexico.

Now in her mid-seventies, she is the matriarch of an expansive family, children and grandchildren whose lives are intricately connected to her and this place. But she is also a volunteer EMT, racing in the dark to an accident in a county twice the size of Rhode Island; she's a leader in the ranching industry, on boards of hospitals and schools. But most of all, she's a working rancher, the one who still rides horseback to tend the land, move the cattle, and work alongside ranch hands who know that she can do anything she asks them to do.

If she was once an anomaly—a girl who was the best cowboy around—she's now become a legend: a sturdy, intense woman who is both role model and final authority. As her grandchildren make their way to the ranch house, there are no big hugs, no grand displays of emotions. There is a large dose of reverence and awe.

"It's hard to explain how enormous our love for her is," says Ryan Davis, her oldest grandson, who is in his twenties. "There's not one of us who wouldn't do anything for her, who doesn't know that we'd be lucky to be half the person our grandma is."

"She is absolutely amazing," says Walter Davis, a grandson still in college.

Linda Davis, Ryan & Walter Davis, Leslie Barmann, Sara & Christiaan Davis

At the ranch in Cimarron, New Mexico (left to right): Linda Davis, Ryan Davis, Sara Davis, Walter Davis, Leslie Barmann, and Christiaan Davis.

Behind a salute or raised hat is a fierce love,
a relationship that the grandchildren describe as profoundly influential,
etched into their actions, their choices,
their sense of the world, and what they can accomplish in it.

"You see so many grandparents who—you know, they love their grand-kids and everything—but no way do they do half the stuff that my grandma is always doing."

Sara Davis, Linda's oldest granddaughter, talks of a recent highlight in their relationship—a visit with her grandmother to the Santa Fe Opera that allowed her to see her grandmother in a larger light.

"There's so much I get just by watching her and the way she talks to people," Sara says. "She never talks down to anyone, and even when we went to the opera—here she has this deep knowledge of opera and I know nothing about it—she's explaining it to me in a way that just makes you want to do more. I've seen that over and over."

Inside the Davis home, every inch of wall and floor is covered with heirlooms: rugs and paintings and photographs that have been in the Davis family since the 1800's, when the ranch was founded. The only item of recent vintage is a serviceable television, which Linda turns on only occasionally to watch a ball game or to catch the opera on PBS.

"This is the core here," Linda says. "The home is the key to the ranch." All of Linda's six children are integral to the ranching operation. Son J. Kirk Davis is the president of the operation. Randolph is in charge of hunting; Bruce is in charge of marketing. Warren and Kim

run separate divisions of the ranch; daughter Julia lives about thirty-five miles away and serves on the state water commission but comes to the ranch daily to look after the animals and treat any that are sick. All of them grew up learning early in their childhood how to ride and rope cat-tle, how to perform tasks that made them feel both competent and responsible for the ranch's welfare.

When the grandchildren were younger, they learned to greet Grandma Linda and Grandpa Les with a firm handshake and a directed gaze. Their grandparents, in turn, treated them as capable beings. Linda made sure that each child had chores, and she never spoke to them as if they were too young to understand the importance of their work.

"She's the kind of person who makes you feel that you're the most important person to her, and it just makes you want to do your best," Walter says.

"I've tried to tell her to slow down, but she won't have that," adds Ryan. "I told her the other day that she shouldn't be running out at three in the morning [as an EMT], and she gave me an ass chewing. She said, 'Ryan, people need my help,' and she shut me down right quick."

"They've been raised with the idea that they have responsibility for the world around them, so they learn from an early age to plan their time, that on a ranch your primary responsibility is to keep the animals and the land healthy," Linda says.

Linda's mother was New Mexico's first public health nurse, legendary for her travels to every remote corner of New Mexico in her bid to inoculate all of the state's children. She was a physically small woman with large ambitions, an expert rider who died when Linda was four.

Her grandmother, who took over Linda's care, was also a legendary horsewoman who rode sidesaddle and laid claim to her own land, using her hands to dig her own well. She was well suited to life on the Tequesquite Ranch that Linda's grandfather built and where Linda and her father lived, eighty-five miles from the nearest town. "She was very versatile, a fantastic lady who always made you feel like you were the most important person in her life. She had the highest standards, and no cowboy sat at her table with spurs or a hat on."

But it was her father, Albert Mitchell, who instilled in Linda a determination to be every bit the cowboy a boy could be, stoic in spirit and willing to do anything: cook for the ranch hands, corral the cattle, find what they needed among the little they had. "The roads were impassable during the winter months, and so we had to lay in our stock of supplies in the fall and then in the spring again," Linda recalls. "We made our own soap, our own lard, and cured the pork in wintertime."

For teachers and friends, she turned to the ranch hands, whom she described as "the best babysitters a girl could have." They taught her to rope, to ride, and to read. She recalls asking the cowboys to read her *Peter Rabbit* so often that she's certain they must have come to hate the story.

By the time she was old enough for college, she'd fallen in love with Les Davis, a young Dartmouth graduate. But her father insisted that she go away to school and learn more about the wider world. At Cornell University, she threw herself into intellectual and artistic stimulation and began a lifelong love affair with opera. But after college, she returned to the ranch and to Les. In 1953, they married.

Throughout her life, Linda's been honored with any number of titles: She's been the head of various state ranching organizations, on the board of the local hospital (sixty miles away), and inducted into the Cowgirl Hall of Fame and the National Cowboy and Western Heritage Museum in Oklahoma City, Oklahoma.

Linda's granddaughter Sara sees in her grandmother a strength and determination that inspires her in a way that all the hugs in the world could not. When Les died, Sara watched her grandmother redouble her efforts on others' behalf, working overtime as an EMT, speaking on behalf of the local hospital, driving a truck to help build a playground for an area school.

"We've all heard it: 'Oh, you're Linda Davis's grandchild?'" Sara says.

Nearly all the older grandchildren envision themselves returning to the ranch. But they know that they'll have to earn their spot; a ranch, no matter how successful, doesn't automatically support all the families that have come from it.

Collectively, they shoulder a weighty legacy; not just to sustain the fortunes of a previous generation, but to rise to the rigors of body and

morality and mind that the Davis legacy represents for them. Who other than their grandmother could have such authority, what grandson Ryan calls "the final of all says."

"I can tell you that just having her name, knowing all that she's done, there's no way any of us want to mess that up," Walter says. "It's always in the back of your mind. There's for sure no way that's going to happen because of something I did."

As one after another of them leave home for college, Linda makes the most of their time back at the ranch. On a day when Walter's parents were out of town, but he was home for a brief break from college, Linda showed up at his door with chowder and a pie, as if she just happened to be in the neighborhood. The one-on-one visits allow her to build the sort of relationship she had with her own grandmother. "Working a ranch, you're very much part of a group, but it's important to see each of them as the individuals they are," Linda notes.

For now, they have gathered against a fence outside the main house. The boys talk of how hard it is to find a girlfriend who even approximates their grandmother. The girls catch up on the latest news of each other's lives. As Linda comes to join them, one of the grandsons tips his hat. Sara tells Linda of her most recent basketball tournament, in which her team came in second. "Who beat you?" Linda wants to know. Then they stand silent for a moment, though just a moment. There's always work to do, and the summer light will only last so long. Squinting into the fading sun, Linda stands straight, the land stretching beyond her to where there are only cows and horses and the broad, proud sky.

Mary Remini looked to the doorway of her New York City apartment where Valerie Johnson seemed to be hesitating.

Valerie was young, in her thirties, from California. Mary had granddaughters in California but it was a foreign land to her.

Mary was a fixture in the building, a recent widow who had lived there for more than fifty years. She was born and raised just a few blocks away, in a neighborhood where she met her husband, worked in a coat factory and raised three boys. Except for ballroom dancing excursions, she rarely ventured beyond Little Italy, or NoLita, as the more gentrified neighborhood was becoming known.

Many of the building's longtime residents were devoted to Mary. They reveled in her quick humor, her storied past, her rough-edged embrace of strangers who quickly became family. Anyone who wanted the apartment would have to first meet Mary.

"Whadsa madder widyou? Nobody's gonna bite ya," Mary said to her.

Thus began a relationship of unlikely proportions. In Valerie, Mary would find an attentive granddaughter; someone who is always there, either in person or by phone. Valerie found in Mary the grandmother she never knew, a woman whose raw edges and life experiences embodied the New York she'd always dreamed she'd find.

"Meeting Mary, I thought, 'This is just the way it's supposed to be.'"

Fifteen years after that first exchange, Val is Mary's devoted companion. As a makeup artist, she often travels on concert tours and with celebrities but checks

Mary Remini &
Valerie Johnson

Valerie Johnson and Mary Remini
chatting in Mary's
New York City living room.

in on Mary at least once a day. They call each other pet names and gush in their phone calls, proclaiming again and again how much they mean to one another.

"She always makes me laugh and has amazing stories," Val says. "She remembers when there were horses on Houston Street, when men used to carry huge blocks of ice up the stairs. It is like having this whole rich history of life right next to you."

They are together for holidays and always on Sundays, the day that Mary makes the rare venture out of her apartment and across the hall to Val's apartment. They eat Chinese food or pizza and watch movies, preferably violent ones. Mary's favorites are about the Mafia. "What she really likes is severe violence, none of this lovey dovey stuff," Val says. "I look for movies where there is no kissing, no dialogue, just violence."

Mary's first son was accidentally shot when he was thirteen and died in her arms. A second son is rarely in touch with her and another died and was cremated before she had a chance to say goodbye. She talks regularly with her two granddaughters in California, one of whom is actress Leah Remini, who stars in the television comedy *The King of Queens*. Leah pays Mary's bills and counts on Val to care for her grandmother in ways she cannot, to protect her from even family members who might take advantage of her declining health. It is Val who has power of attorney over Mary's affairs, Val who knows what Mary has eaten on a given day, or, lately, if she's eaten anything at all.

"If I'm away, I worry so much about her," Val says. "When I call, she always says, 'Your ears must be ringing. I tell everybody about how much I love you.' And I always say, 'Mary, you know that I feel the same way.' "

Mary grew up in a Little Italy that was then known for its underworld ties. Her father died when she was young and her understanding of the world did not extend far beyond the few blocks outside her door. By the time she met her husband ("the worst kind of man to marry") she still did not understand where babies came from. The couple moved into Mary's current building and Mary took a job at a clothing factory on Broadway. "I was a wizard—a wizard I tell you," she says. "The Jewish man I worked for was so disappointed when I left."

Mary is proud to show a visitor her apartment, with its imitation-brick wallpaper, its stovetop iron, the window where Mary has always loved to take in the view. She used to watch the comings and goings of Mafia figures and their lookout cars; now she gazes down Elizabeth Street at the upwardly-mobile couples coming and going from trendy shops and restaurants.

The view represents the New York where Val and Mary's life intersect, though Val's route there was nothing like Mary's. She was raised in San Marino by two loving parents in a palatial home. Val's father was a veterinarian who brought home abandoned animals. Val's mother was a favorite among her friends. "My best friend from childhood was the youngest of eight and kind of forgotten. She says to this day that my parents are responsible for the person she has become."

Still, there were voids in her life. Val rarely saw her maternal grandparents. Her father's parents had died by the time Val was a teenager. And though her home was a happy one, Val craved a life more stimulating than her sterile suburban surroundings would allow, and she dreamed she would find such a world in New York.

"I always wanted to live in an apartment building like Lucy and Ethel. I watched *Breakfast at Tiffany's* and *Midnight Cowboy* and *Annie Hall*. I had this fixation about going to New York."

Even though Mary was a native New Yorker, it was Val who introduced Mary to New York landmarks and people. When Val had an event associated with singer Judy Collins, whom she assisted for many years, she'd convince Mary to come along. She brought her to Carnegie Hall and the Russian Tea Room, where Mary met Paul Newman and former Mayor David Dinkins.

At the time, Mary was a regular writer of opinion letters to the *New York Daily News*. Once, attending a gala with Val, she spied the mayor and made a bee-line for him, armed with a bevy of complaints. "He was totally enchanted," Val recalls.

But that seems like a long time ago now. At ninety-two, Mary almost never leaves her apartment. She's lost some of the vigor and weight that made her appear robust even as little as six months ago. She no longer goes out to have her hair done up in a beehive, a fact that saddens Val, though

she is heartened when Mary talks about an appointment, as if the salon visits are only on temporary hiatus. Yet, earlier this year, when Val was in the hospital for surgery, Mary tried to make it down the stairs by herself, fell, and injured her hip and back.

Now, when she greets a visitor she is unable to conceal her pain. On a day when Val is in California, Mary counts the days until Val returns. "She loves me like you have no idea," Mary says. "There is not a day she don't call. Every night when I go to sleep, I say, 'My God, hurry up and make her come home.' "

Increasingly, Mary is becoming forgetful, having a harder time getting around. Val arranges for visits from Meals on Wheels, for doctor's appointments, and for deliveries from grocery stores. Mary's granddaughters in California urge her to move there. But she won't hear of it.

"I don't want nobody to tell me what to do, what not to do, don't sit here, don't sit there," she says. "I love my house. I've been living here almost seventy-five years."

And in Val, she has her own piece of California right next door.

"I got so many good people in my life, I don't have time for the bad ones," she says. "Did I tell you that I call Val my daughter? I miss her so much but I know she's coming home to me."

It's not that she had anything against the idea of being a grandmother, it's just that

Joan Logghe didn't see herself in that role; not yet anyway.

She'd just buried her mother-in-law. Her own mother, she'd just learned, had a month to live. And now she had to break the news to her daughter, Corina. But as she talked of her mother's illness, she realized as she looked at Corina that her daughter had some news of her own.

"You're pregnant, aren't you?" she asked Corina.

"How did you know?" Corina was only a few weeks along.

Joan sighed. Perhaps it was destiny. Joan had named Corina after "Corrina's Going A-Maying," a poem about love, about young maidens celebrating May Day by taking a tumble with a village lad. They agreed that since Corina wasn't married (she'd only been dating her boyfriend for a short time), they'd keep the news from Joan's mother. But it wasn't Corina's marital state that so weighed on Joan's mind.

Corina was twenty-seven, just starting her career as an artist, painting scarves. Joan was fifty-five. She'd never thought of her daughter as a mother and certainly didn't see herself as a grandmother. She still had a sixteen-year-old at home. Her husband, Mike, would soon leave his job. And in this year filled with so much death, it was hard to imagine that she would recover her spirits through a new baby.

As a poet and teacher, Joan was in the business of words, and now she tried to discern what the word *grandmother* brought to mind. Both of Joan's grandmothers had died before she was born. She had friends who proclaimed the glory of grandmotherhood, who insisted that it was the best thing in the world. But Joan couldn't help but wonder: If being a grandmother was so great, why

Joan Logghe, Corina Logghe & Galen Haynes

was the big advantage supposed to be that you could give the kid back?

And in truth, Joan knew plenty of grandmothers in the La Puebla neighborhood where she'd raised Corina who never gave the kids back. They were the caregivers while their children went to work or pursued careers. Well, that wasn't going to be Joan. "Don't expect me to be one of those grandparents," she told Corina. "I've already raised my kids."

"Oh, you're so cute, Mom," Corina told her, and Joan thought, *Cute? I'm fifty-five and already you see me as a cute old lady?* When she was a new mother herself, Joan had thought that no image was less romantic than that of a woman pushing a shopping cart with a child in tow. Now she was "cute"? Grandmotherly cute? Talk about being desexualized.

Joan did what she always did when she was trying to puzzle out life's transitions: She wrote about it. She couldn't get away from the connotation that swirled around the very term *grandmother*. It brought to mind images that were either oversentimentalized or oversimplified. "I feel older than I've ever been," she told her husband, Mike.

Mike laughed. Hadn't she always loved wearing those baggy, frumpy clothes? "You've been old since I met you," Mike teased.

As the pregnancy progressed, Joan could see that Corina was over the moon. The father-to-be was just twenty-five, an artist too, and they seemed happy together, sharing with Joan their latest baby-in-utero stories.

They decided to deliver the baby in their new house, with three midwives and appropriate music. As is the norm for a new-age New Mexican, Corina had taken the baby to be "channeled." The channeler had predicted that the baby would be a healer or a visionary. Joan couldn't help but yawn. *Why is it they never tell you your baby is going to be a mediocre algebra teacher?* she thought.

More than anything, Joan was struck by the irony of the timing. It had been a year of so many deaths, of September 11, of losses both large and small. Over time, the prospect of Corina's baby carried an aura of badly needed hope. Joan found herself talking about the baby more than she would have imagined. She told the dry cleaner and the grocer. She shared her news with the FedEx guy, who asked whether it was a girl or a boy. Joan explained that Corina wanted a natural birth and didn't see a need for ultrasound. "You would have thought I'd said she wasn't going to have prenatal care," she later told Mike.

The call came in the middle of the night. During the drive to Corina's house, Joan imagined herself a tourist, for isn't that what she was? A visitor to a realm of motherhood where she wouldn't remain?

But once she arrived, she knew this was where she was supposed to be. Corina had always been beautiful, but in a willowy way that gave her an air of vulnerability. Now, watching her in childbirth, Joan saw a woman of enormous strength, resolve, and peace that told Joan that this was right, this baby at this time.

His name is Galen. And now that he's nearing two, Joan can tell you a few things about becoming "Ama." For starters, there's the physical longing she has if she doesn't see him for more than seven days. "It's this chemical thing," she says. "I'm addicted to him. I'm not kidding." There's the crazy-in-love feeling that is not so different from the loony love that led her to marry Mike so many years ago. (And Mike is equally smitten with Galen, but that's another story.)

And like any relationship, it is infinitely nuanced. "It's not like I'm the adoring grandmother and he's the perfect baby," she laughs. "He's fourteen months, but he's starting to show independence, which is so hard on me. Corina keeps saying, 'Oh, you need to get on the floor with him.' And I realize that I'm acting like a spurned lover, working out all my unrequited love affairs."

So now, when she hears the term *grandma*, what does it bring to mind? Joan describes a role that is so rich and layered that it defies easy categorization. "You'll see some ridiculous story: Here's the modern grandma running a marathon. Here's the stereotypical grandmother. But just like every single person, every single story, there is so much more to the relationship."

Whatever it is, Joan is smitten. Though she carries pictures, she dwells on his tiniest accomplishments ("He's found his thumb! He can say 'Ma!' ").

She marvels that in this bond, which is so often trivialized or oversimplified, she is finding one of the richest relationships she's known.

"In this one relationship is all of the complexity of human life," she says gleefully. "And it's just wild if you pay attention."

On a bright day in 1984, Alexis Abramson went to Florida
to visit her grandmother, who had recently taken a new job.

Alexis was a college sophomore then, a striking brunette with Elizabeth Taylor eyes whose bon vivant spirit seemed a perfect match for the tourism industry in which she planned to work. She'd always been spontaneous, the fun-loving daughter in a family of determined doctors.

Alexis had only recently become close to her grandmother, Rose. As a child, Alexis had viewed Rose (or Mimi, as she calls her) as if she were from another world, a place Alexis went only on holidays or vacations. But as she grew older, leaving her home in Macon, Georgia, for school in Arizona, Alexis found herself drawn more and more to this woman who spoke to her so honestly, and with such optimism, about even the most difficult relationships and choices.

At sixty-eight, recently widowed, Rose had set out for a new life. After having devoted her life to her husband and his medical practice, she found what she was looking for at the University of Florida, as a housemother for the Delta Phi Epsilon sorority there. Her world, which had once seemed so foreign to Alexis, began to look more and more like the one in which Alexis was living.

It occurred to Alexis, as she made her way to the university and then up the steps of her grandmother's sorority house, that what brought her to this place were questions about her future. Her grandmother had come to this place as a way to move on from the past.

Rose Holtzman

Alexis Abramson

Rose Holtzman and Alexis Abramson
in the bedroom of Rose's home
in Atlanta, Georgia.

89

The grandmother whom Alexis saw that weekend was hardly burdened by sadness. "It was pretty amazing to see her charisma and intellect and femininity and grace come through, to see the respect and awe these girls had for her, how they valued every single word and came to her room at all times of the night for advice," Alexis says. "I so appreciated her as a role model. I think that was a turning point for me, to see her in her glory, surrounded by all these girls and having this wonderful exchange.

"It wasn't that others had to see her value before I could, too," she adds. "It just became very tangible; I could really see her wisdom, and it made me thirst for more of the relationship. I had this feeling that I need to cherish each moment."

In the months and years that followed, Alexis and Rose have built a relationship that both celebrates their age difference and seems to defy it. Rose inspired Alexis to search for a career that was more meaningful, which ultimately led to her acclaimed work in gerontology. Her grandmother was the first to see in Alexis 'a special gift,' something unique that she could offer a segment of society that needed it badly. "Don't waste your talent," she told Alexis.

Now thirty-seven, Alexis is the creator of a multi-million dollar company that connects senior citizens with products that make their lives easier. She's also a speaker and consultant, just completed her Ph.D. in gerontology, is the author of *The Caregiver's Survival Handbook*, and has been a guest on NBC's *Today* show. Not bad for someone who Rose once worried would be "a bad seed."

"You know what she called me?" Alexis says, sprawled on the floor of her grandmother's apartment. Rose, in a chair next to her, is ninety-two, living on her own in an assisted-living center that looks more like a luxury condominium. "She called me 'that crumb.'"

"But she really has changed," Rose says with a half laugh. "One day, her grandmother and I were sitting and talking and this one, she flew down the steps with a few of her friends and didn't say a word to us . . ."

"You didn't like my friends," Alexis notes.

"Her friends were not really nice girls," Rose whispers.

"They were nice girls," Alexis says. "They were just a little rambunctious, a little on the wild side. I don't think we were disrespectful. I think we were just not cognizant, not aware."

"Right," Rose says. "You didn't know we existed." Rose waves a hand at Alexis's protestations, "Anyway, we were talking—her other grandmother and I—and she just walked by and didn't say a word. Not hello, nothing, and Esther said to me, 'Rose,' she said, 'is that our granddaughter?' You know, you'd think maybe we'd hear a 'good morning' . . ."

"I was young," Alexis protests. "And I said good morning. Anyway, the net of this is that I realized your value a little bit later. Is that what you're saying? Like when I went to college and you'd visit. Remember how drunk you'd get off those margaritas?"

Rose raises her eyebrows. "Let's not talk about that."

From the time Alexis began her company in 1995 Rose was a vital member of the team, where Phyllis, Alexis's mother and Phyllis's daughter, worked, too. Rose answered phones (sometimes juggling six lines at a time), wrote a column for the company's website, and on more than a

What Rose wanted for Alexis—
more than a boyfriend or marriage or even the love of her life—
was that she'd become a woman on her own terms,
living to the fullest of her potential.

few occasions provided the color for interviewers who were profiling Alexis and her company.

On her 86th birthday, for example, Rose did a live interview with National Public Radio while baking a cake. The host expected to hear her views on aging, but first heard her open the oven door, pull out the pan and yell, "Wait, just let me turn the oven off."

The interview was vintage Rose, who squeezes what she can out of even small interactions. "I believe very strongly—I tell Alexis this—that nothing should be left undone and nothing should be left unsaid."

The walls of Rose's apartment on Peachtree Street, in the heart of Atlanta, are lined with pictures of her family: her four grandchildren, her two daughters, her parents, and her life growing up in the Catskill Mountains of upstate New York. There are also photographs and mementos from the women who passed through the sorority where Rose worked until she was eighty-three; she still hears from those women, who might call to talk about a divorce or their children's marriage. There are even photos of students she taught during her early married days as a first-grade teacher; some of them are in their seventies now.

Alexis surveys the images. "I have a very, very close relationship with both of my parents," she says, "but my grandmother is in her nineties,

and she's seen history repeat itself over and over and over. Her sense of worldliness and understanding of what my expectations can be, having lived through so many periods of time, makes me truly try to embody and listen to everything she says and take it very much to heart."

Rose lived with her husband in South Fallsburg, New York, where he was the town doctor. He delivered most of the town's babies, making house calls or seeing patients in a small office attached to their house. Rose kept track of the appointments and finances and served as an ad hoc therapist, talking with patients and their families while they waited to see her husband.

When he died, she closed up the house and went to school to learn how to write a résumé. For two years, she could not find a job until her daughter, Phyllis, saw an ad for a housemother at the sorority. She took it, and began a chapter of her life that was rewarding in ways she never expected.

"You know, the fifteen years I spent there were the happiest of my life," Rose says. "I think when you're happy like that, it shows. You have a sense of humor about life."

Alexis was also coming into her own during those years. Rose told her often that she needed to get all the wisdom she could, to absorb lessons everywhere, from college classes, from good and bad relationships, from

even the smallest interactions. That was the first part of her job. The second part was even more important—to give that wisdom back.

At the time, Alexis was still pursuing a career in the tourism industry and had an internship at a Club Med in the British West Indies. One day a week was senior night, when the staff was to entertain the senior citizens who were visiting the club. While her coworkers dreaded those evenings, Alexis relished them, moving from person to person, absorbing their life stories and anecdotes. She wasn't put off by the physicality of aging—wrinkled skin or debilitating conditions—nor was she frightened about coming face to face with mortality, the way her colleagues were.

One day, when she was in New York on a family trip, she caught sight of an elderly woman crossing the street just as a car made its way toward the intersection. "For the hundredth time, I went running out into the street because I was worried that she was going to be hit," she says, "and I remember this moment where I was standing there and the light changed and I was thinking, *Why is no one else moving?*"

The experience made urgent an idea she'd been mulling over: to devote herself to making life better for people of her grandparents' generation. She'd once worked with seniors at the Jewish Community Center of Greater Atlanta and had witnessed there a woman struggling to make a phone call because she couldn't see the telephone dial and a devoted reader unable to see the page because he couldn't hold a magnifying glass. But she discovered that it was not easy even for her to locate a hands-free magnifying glass or a phone dial large enough to serve seniors who were struggling to see.

At twenty-eight, she borrowed $50,000, turned down a scholarship to get a Ph.D., and started her own company, providing products that made seniors' lives easier. Two years later, Mature Mart had sales of $3 million. Rose, who'd retired from her job at the sorority, joined Alexis, working for her company four days a week.

In summoning the courage to start the company, Alexis drew in part on her grandmother's determination to make a life for herself after her husband died. And what Rose wanted for Alexis—more than a boyfriend or marriage or even the love of her life—was that she'd become a woman on her own terms, living to the fullest of her potential.

"I think you learned a lot by seeing me when I was alone and took a job," Rose tells Alexis."

"Absolutely," Alexis says. "That's why I gave you a third job at Mature Mart."

The experience of working together has added yet another dimension to their relationship and, with it, their individual sense of self.

"Our relationship is not superficial at all, and I think that's the difference between us and a lot of grandparents and grandchildren," Alexis says. "With a lot of people, you love each other, but you don't necessarily get the person. You understand the shell of the person, but a lot of times you don't understand the soul. We see each other from the inside out rather than from the outside in. I see myself in Mimi, and I think she sees herself in me."

They find the grave, crouch at its edge.

"Who's that, Destiny? Is that Mommy?"

Destiny traces the letters with her fingers, balancing herself against her grandmother's knees.

"You want to say a prayer?" Tawana Colon bows her shoulders, bearing the weight of a generation's loss. "Our father in heaven, thank you for giving me another day to visit my daughter's final resting place. Her soul belongs to you now. Let her watch over her daughter. And thank you for the blessing of Destiny."

Tawana Colon is both grandmother and mother, a soldier in a war of maternal defiance. She raised her four children in one of D.C.'s toughest neighborhoods, determined to fight the assumptions that poor kids are fated to lives with little education, dead-end jobs, and limited futures. Her children would study hard. Her kids would go to college. Nothing would keep her kids from getting out of the neighborhood, from building better lives.

By Mother's Day, 2002, Tawana had every reason to celebrate. Her older daughter, Tysha, was a track star on scholarship first at George Mason University and then at Seton Hall. Her son, Isaac, wrote poetry that had taken him to Brazil and to the White House, where he had read for President Bill Clinton. Her younger daughter and namesake, Tawana, was an honor student.

Two months earlier, her middle child, Shirlita—or Shirley as her mother calls her—had given birth to a baby girl. Shirley was just a baby herself—barely fifteen—and when she told her mother that she was pregnant, Tawana vowed that the baby would not derail her daughter's future. She would look upon this grandchild as a new beginning, not the end of her daughter's education and life.

Tawana Colon
& Destiny Colon

Tawana Colon and Destiny Colon
at Shirley's grave near Tawana's home
in Washington, D.C.

Shirley was the family cutup who dreamed of being a designer. Tawana was barely forty, a small-framed woman with a passion for raising children. In the apartment building where the Colons lived, Tawana was everyone's mother. Neighborhood kids inevitably made their way to her home, calling her Aunt Tiny and, eventually, Grandma.

On February 28, 2002, Destiny was born. Ten weeks later, Shirley met with Destiny's father, apparently asking him for money to buy diapers. Not long after that meeting, he lured her to the back of a nearby church and shot her dead.

In the months that followed, Destiny and Tawana clung to each other, both desperate to hold the mother and child now buried in the ground. Destiny cried incessantly, for so long and in such pain, that Tawana took her to the hospital emergency room, in search of something that would comfort her granddaughter. "This poor child was a breast-fed baby, and all she wanted was her mother," Tawana says. "For me, there were days I wished I'd just not wake up."

In Destiny, Tawana found the will to live. "I can't replace Shirley, and I know that," Tawana says. "But Destiny needs me; my children need me. Hate and anger won't do nothing but make you sick. This child, she's the most precious thing God could have given me. What I can do is give this child all the love I can. Her story is so horrible, and someday she's going to know that. But what I can do is show her that she is so beautiful, that she is Destiny, and she is this huge blessing."

In the apartment where Tawana and her family moved after Shirley's death, there is a wall covered with pictures. There's Tysha on the track, with medals draped around her neck. There's Isaac standing next to former President Bill Clinton. And there's Shirley, hand on her hip, head tipped back in laughter, flashing a smile for the camera.

Destiny at age two is a whirl of motion, climbing on and off her grandma's lap, retrieving one book, then another, pointing to the pictures with a two-year-old's hunger to name what she sees. "This?"

"That's Barney," Tawana tells her.

"This?"

"That's a cow. How does a cow go?"

"Mooo," Destiny proclaims proudly.

"She reminds me so much of Shirley," Tawana says. "She is just so full of life."

The last time Tawana saw Shirley was early on Mother's Day. Tawana was on the apartment balcony, sharing a toast with a friend. Shirley and Tysha waved to their mother from below. "Those daughters of yours sure are pretty," her friend said, loudly enough for the girls to hear. Shirley copped a pose, bathing in her mother's admiration. And then the girls were down the street and out of sight.

Later that night, after a celebratory dinner with her husband, Tawana was on her way back to their apartment when she turned the corner and saw a crowd gathered near the church. She recognized faces and saw in them something that sent shock waves through her blood. "Please don't let it be mine," she remembers saying. "Please, Lord, don't let it be one of mine." But even as she said this, she knew.

In that moment, Tawana was admitted to an ever-growing club of grandparents who are taking up the burden of their lost children.

"We as a generation must step in," she says. "These kids, you see them just give up on school, on life. It's so hard on them now, and they have to know they have someone strong behind them. That's what I've always told my kids, that no matter what happened, I would support them."

"Here comes Tawana with someone else's baby," was a refrain Tawana remembers hearing as a child. She was an aunt by age three, raised with the help of a grandmother and a mother who put their church at the center of their lives. By eight or nine, she was caring for other people's children and close to her own grandmother, who told her that children were a blessing and a responsibility, that a mother's role was to put her children's interests before her own.

While raising Destiny, Tawana is also helping raise Tysha's daughter while Tysha finishes college. Recently, Tysha told her mom that she was going to pay her back, that when she graduated and got a job, that would be the first thing she did. Tawana told her, "You finishing college, succeeding, that's all the payment I need."

The larger challenge Tawana knows will come as Destiny grows up and learns about her parents. Her mother is dead. Her father is in jail. At some point, Tawana knows, Destiny will have to absorb that.

"She might grow up and want to see her father," Tawana says. "Right now, I just keep telling her that her momma's watching over her, and I believe that. Sometimes, I'll be watching her and she'll do something so cute, and I think, *Oh, I wish Shirley could see that,* and then I think, she can see her. She's right here with me."

Often, when they are at the cemetery, Destiny makes games of chasing geese or catching butterflies. But today, she stays near Tawana, clinging to her hand, watching her grandmother while Tawana prays: "Lord, thank you for the blessing of Destiny. Thank you for each day that you allow her to come and visit her mother's grave, and God, I wish that you would keep all the violence and all the crime out of my family and the lives of others around me. Help us to make this world a better place so tragedies like this will not happen again. In Jesus' name I pray. Amen."

Destiny is silent.

"Say, 'Amen,' " Tawana says gently.

Destiny smiles up at her grandmother, then runs her finger over the lettering of her mother's name and whispers, "Amen."

On the eve of a man's birthday,
He is entitled to a moment of reflection.

He may be particularly reflective if, by that birthday, he has attained a position of leadership once occupied by his grandfather and great- grandfather —a position he owes in part to his grandmother. And if that man is Rabbi Naftali Citron, and his grandmother is, among other things, his boss, that reflection has little chance of lasting a mere moment.

"I'm just following the tradition of breaking out; breaking loose, so to speak, doing my own thing," Naftali says as he muses. He and his grandmother, Hadassa Carlebach, are in his office at The Carlebach Shul, a small but famous synagogue on New York's West 79th Street. His grandmother is the treasurer and a trustee of the synagogue where she remains a powerful tie to the past. As wife to one of the congregation's late rabbis and sister-in-law to another, she was a key organizing force inside the synagogue and a warm pastoral touch beyond it.

For Naftali, she is an inspiration, a woman who, as a teenager, hid orphans from the Nazis. As a grandmother, she was an important bridge between the more rigid, traditional world that Naftali's mother created for him and the more liberal Judiasm that was practiced at his grandparent's shul. It is a role that fed the philosophies at the core of his rabbinical life.

"What I really like to do is bridge the gap that exists between the secular and the religious, between the outside and the inside, between the external form of religion and the internal spiritual experience. I mean, I relate

Hadassa
Carlebach
& Naftali Citron

Naftali Citron and Hadassa Carlebach
at her kitchen table
in Brooklyn, New York.

better to the nonreligious person who says, 'Explain this to me,' than the religious person who says, 'Tell me the law. Is this kosher?' The reason I ended up at this synagogue is because both my grandfather and my great-uncle did this really cool stuff and they were relating to people who didn't fit the mold.

Hadassa saw early on that her grandson had an unusual ability to share ideas and reach people.

"He was able to take this very complicated material—very, very complex—and go beyond the facts and get into the spirit, the meaning of it. But then, he could *explain* it. I was amazed. "You know," she says, "there are a lot of smart people who understand things that are very complicated. But if you're not able to communicate it, if you are not able to make it palatable so that people understand what this spirituality is all about. Then maybe the knowledge is good for your own ego, but it is not really helping those around you."

Naftali has heard this before. "Did she mention that I sing also?"

"I'd rather you not sing," Hadassa says. "Not yet. Take a few lessons."

"See!" Naftali gestures toward her. "It is not always like, 'You are the greatest.' It's like, 'You speak well, but your singing needs work.'"

Naftali's great uncle was the famed composer poser Shlomo Carlebach, who in the 1960s played with the likes of Pete Seeger and Bob Dylan and created the House of Love and Prayer, reaching to lost souls with his own brand of Judiasm. He joined his brother, Eli Chaim, Naftali's grandfather, and

together they built a spirited congregation at the Carlebach Shul.

The synagogue's services drew an unusual assortment of worshipers—women in jeans next to men with long beards and black hats. The place and its liberalism appealed to young Naftali.

But he was raised in a strict Orthodox home and attended a Yeshiva, a Jewish school where boys and girls did not mix and where his social life was restricted; he could not go into places like a local pizza parlor where teenagers hung out. His seemingly mild form of rebellion—spending more and more time with his paternal grandparents and in their congregation—was, for his mother, anything but benign.

"I was so able to talk things over with my grandmother, important things, decisions that had to be made, things like that," he says. "And again, sometimes you can't relate to your parents or can't tell them everything."

At his grandparents' synagogue, he found an openness and a level of inquiry that fed his spirit and mind. But his mother did not like the sort of openness that she saw there.

"Here was my great-uncle, this holy hippie, who hugged and kissed all the women, and my mother was petrified. She certainly didn't see him as a role model. But I did, and my grandmother had to fight with my mother to let me come here."

"Grandparents," Naftali says, "because they are a little bit removed, they have the same love but they . . ."

"They don't have to fix all the mistakes," Hadassa says.

"They don't have those neuroses," he says. "The parents may be like, 'Oh, my son became a rabbi. What did I do wrong?' But a grandparent can see this other perspective which is like, 'Hey, this kid has something,' and maybe this is not exactly what the parent would like to see. I think there is a certain closeness between parents and their children that colors their perspective. Of course parents say they really want the child to have what's best for him or her—they pay lip service to that—but there is a lack of distance, and that lack of distance doesn't always allow them to see all the nuances of the child."

On the walls of Naftali's office are large portraits of his great uncle, his grandfather, and his great-grandfather Naphtali, who was named rabbi of the congregation in 1950.

The current Naftali was just thirty-one when he was named the congregation's rabbi in 2003. In the context of his large legacy, Hadassa's role as a board member and treasurer and her guidance became even more important.

"In any business you have to have that one person you trust, the person you know is not going to try to use what's going on to gain power or for monetary gain or to do anything but watch out for you and tell you what's wrong and needs to be fixed," Naftali says.

Hadassa considers this comment and wonders aloud about what

Hassidic masters would say if asked when one person has the right to criticize another. "Isn't it that in order to chastise or criticize someone, that if you don't really love them or care about them, you can't criticize them?"

"I think Dale Carnegie said that," Naftali says.

"No, really. Unless you love the person very deeply, you can't criticize them."

Naftali ponders this, the amusing self-help guru Dale Carnegie versus the Hassidic teachers. "Carnegie would tell you to first compliment them."

"But that's manipulation," Hadassa notes. "That's different."

This is a typical exchange for Hadassa and her grandson, where an occasional comment becomes a penetrating examination of the opportunities and limitations of any religion.

"Like everything else, a religion has to have a structure," Naftali says. "But structure can also shade, it can conceal and hide, keep people from asking, 'What's the inner meaning?'"

"When you are dealing with a tradition—and this is so like a relationship with a grandparent—the tradition has to have both depth and life all in the same root," Naftali adds. "The depth is you are going back, maybe a thousand, three thousand, years. But there has to be life so that it can

rejuvenate. That is the secret of a real tradition, a tradition that does not become petrified and then turn into fundamentalism. That is the secret of a relationship with a grandparent—a secret brought to life in the relationship he shares with Hadassa.

Hadassa never knew her own grandmother. She was raised in France and came of age during the Nazi occupation. At thirteen, she worked with her father along with the French resistance, hiding groups of orphans in the French Alps and risking her own life to find medicine or food or lead a young child to an outhouse. The Nazis captured her mother carrying pictures of Hadassa and her father, but her mother survived torture and never gave up her daughter's location.

"I look at what my mother did, and I think, *Could I have done that?*" Hadassa asks. "Could I have held out?"

Naftali grew up knowing the broad outlines of Hadassa's story, as well as that of his maternal grandmother, who was a Holocaust survivor.

But as he listens to his grandmother, he is struck once again by the power she has to inspire and guide him. "There is this way in which she is this amazing role model for me," he says. "The heroic thing—that of course I always admired. But there is a more practical lesson. You don't have to wait until you are a hundred years old to take responsibility for your life."

So they return to the original question: Who has the right to criticize another person. Eventually, they agree on the Hassidic interpretation:

You must love somebody the way a parent loves a child in order to criticize someone purely, with no motive other than love.

"See this is what our relationship is about," Naftali says, "getting to the core of things. How do you know what love is? What is a tradition? I have my grandmother to tell me these things."

There is a pause and the recognition that the sky has gone dark, that most everyone in the small building has left. Naftali talks of dinner, of whether Hadassa will join his wife and two young sons, who will be waiting to celebrate his thirty-third birthday.

"He makes the best martinis," Hadassa exclaims. "And he can cook!'

Returning to the conversation at hand, she reminds her grandson of a story, then, as if she doesn't remember it, asks him, "How does that go?"

Naftali obliges. "One of the Hassidic masters, a very simple-seeming person but very profound at the same time, he used to say that when I die and leave this world and come to the heavenly court, they are not going to ask me, 'How come you weren't as great as Moses, how come you didn't study as much or weren't as generous as Abraham or as strict as Isaac or as sacrificing as Jacob?' "

"They are going to say, 'How come you weren't as great as you could have been?' "

"You see," Hadassa says as she rises to leave. As if to say that at least for tonight, she is rewarded by her grandson, by the fact of him, that for now, her work is done.

Stephanie Valdez was on her grandmother's floor; her grandmother, Corinne, was on the couch behind her.

They were doing their usual dinner-movie thing. At twenty-five, Stephanie was a mother, an adult, but when she was at her grandmother's house north of Dallas, she felt as if she were seven years old.

Stephanie had brought along her jewelry and figured she'd work on a few pieces while the two of them chatted. Jewelrymaking was a new venture, something she'd picked up from customers at the craft store where she had a part-time job. Her mother Marilyn, Corinne's daughter, saw Stephanie's efforts as more of a hobby, something that might take her mind off her pending divorce or financial pressures. But then, Stephanie and her mother had always approached life differently.

Marilyn was barely eighteen when Stephanie was born, and Stephanie had always felt inadequate in her mother's shadow. Her mother was tall, thin, and stunning, even if she did favor clothes that Stephanie found hopelessly conservative. Next to her, Stephanie felt lumpish and awkward. "Someday, you'll be as beautiful as your mother," people would always say, and Stephanie would feel a rage that tore her apart.

But in her grandmother, Stephanie found a kindred soul. They both loved fashion; they loved makeup and jewelry. Corinne had worked much of her adult life as a banker, an accomplishment of which she was deeply proud. She was the oldest daughter of divorced parents; her father raised the children and counted on Corinne as if she were the mother. Though

Corinne Gonzales
& Stephanie
Valdez

Corrine Gonzales and Stephanie Valdez
share a laugh at Maribella's
in Dallas, Texas.

she had skipped two grades, she never made it to college but instead cared for the family.

When Stephanie was little and her parents divorced, her grandmother became her refuge. When at age six, her father died suddenly, it seemed right that she'd move to her grandmother's house for a time. Stephanie knew girls whose grandmothers were their second mothers. But for Stephanie, Corinne was more than that. "It was such a terrible time when my dad passed away. My grandmother filled a big hole. She made me feel so comfortable, so good just to be me."

Now, as Stephanie faced financial uncertainty and the prospect of raising two children on her own, she turned again to the haven that her grandmother had always provided. Her mother wanted Stephanie to find her own way. She told her mother that as a grandmother the best thing she could do for Stephanie was to step back and allow her to fall.

But as Corinne gazed at her granddaughter, she saw a young woman in search of the vehicle to express her extraordinary talent. This grandchild had passion and soul. Corinne loved her with *lastima;* she loved her so much it hurt.

Stephanie poured the jewelry from her bag, separating fragments of stones and metal from the dozen pieces that she'd already finished. Her grandmother took one look and nearly shouted with delight. "Stephanie! Those are beautiful!"

Corinne couldn't believe what she saw. From a pile of discarded metals and semi-precious stones, her granddaughter had crafted pieces unlike anything she had seen. They blended the old and new, with a sophistication about them that commanded the eye.

She could barely contain herself. "Oh, this is it. You have found your calling." She ran to get a camera while Stephanie protested that she looked terrible.

"Nonsense," her grandmother said. "I'm taking a picture of a young woman who is going to be a great, great success."

The next day, Corinne called her daughter. "Stephanie's really onto something here," she told Marilyn. She'd decided to invite over some of her women friends to allow Stephanie to show off her stuff. Marilyn was touched by her mother's efforts on Stephanie's behalf. She knew she couldn't convince her mother to back off, and certainly she wanted her daughter to succeed.

Besides, Marilyn was reeling from changes in her own life. She'd been laid off after fifteen years as an executive for a fragrance firm. At forty-five, she suddenly didn't know who she was. She thought about her own grandmother, Stephanie's great-grandmother, "the greatest diva of them all." Her grandmother cared deeply about fashion and beauty and always imagined that Marilyn would have a store.

Marilyn decided to open Maribella's, a boutique with one-of-a-kind accessories. A few weeks before the April, 2001, opening of the store, Corinne called with more stories about Stephanie's jewelry. Stephanie had only been creating her own pieces for a few months, but in that short time, her grandmother had seen how people had responded to it. Everyone who saw it wanted to buy it.

Marilyn figured she'd encourage Stephanie to bring a few pieces of her jewelry to the store for the opening, as a way for the family to celebrate the opening together.

The night of the opening, Maribella's was stocked with handbags and wallets, belts and jewelry, including the pieces that Stephanie had made. Marilyn reveled in the four generations that were represented there: Her mother, her daughter, and her granddaughter, Isabella. But it was Stephanie who surprised her the most. She positively glowed, and Marilyn was delighted to watch her daughter so at ease with customers; and the customers were drawn to her and her work.

They peppered Marilyn with questions: Where did the jewelry come from? What inspired it? Is there more?

At that moment, Marilyn knew that she was meant to open this store, but not for herself. "I'll never forget looking at Stephanie," says Marilyn. "She was so radiant, so beautiful, and I just felt so proud of her. I thought, *It's her time.* I thought opening the store was going to be about something totally different, about me. But I remember thinking, *This is my time to help Stephanie. That's what this store is about.*"

Four years later, Stephanie's jewelry sells for upwards of $1,000 a piece. The store is mainly supported by those sales, a fact that delights Marilyn who, along with Corinne, is Stephanie's biggest booster. The venture has transformed their relationship. "We work so well together," Stephanie says. "We just enjoy each other in a way we never could. We've become two parts of a whole; one of us could not succeed without the other."

"There is no way Maribella's would exist without her," Marilyn says. "You know, we hope as mothers that our children will become whole,

Corinne gazed at her granddaughter, she saw what she'd always seen: a young woman in search of the vehicle to express her extraordinary talent. This grandchild had passion and soul. Corinne loved her with *lastima;* she loved her so much it hurt.

complete, and I wanted that for Stephanie. But I always sort of doubted it would happen because of all her struggles. My mother never doubted it. Not for a second. I'd say, 'You know, Mom, I think we need to let Stephanie go, let her fly on her own.' My mother absolutely refused to do that."

Stephanie takes it a step further. "If my grandmother had not let me be who I was during those years, if she hadn't loved me no matter who I was, I know I would not be the person I am today. I'd have nowhere near the kind of confidence I have."

As Stephanie has matured in her craft, Marilyn has found even deeper rewards in her role as grandmother to Isabella and Stephanie's four-year-old son. "The other day," says Stephanie, "I heard my grandmother say to my mom, 'See. Now you understand what it feels like, that love.'"

Marilyn laughs with recognition. "Oh gosh, you know, you love those grandchildren like there is no tomorrow. I used to get upset with my mother for the relationship she had with Stephanie, the way she'd always take her point of view. I wanted her to back me up. She'd always say that she was neutral, but her actions were always on behalf of Stephanie.

"Now I understand. I love those kids with, with *lastima*. I don't know how else to explain it. I know they are going to go through bumpy roads.

I know what's ahead for them. But you just never would let them go."

There's an image that Stephanie likes to recall. She's sitting cross-legged in her pajamas atop the huge bed with its red velvet headboard. Her grandmother hands her a box. It is black and shiny with gold flecks that are wearing away.

Stephanie knows what is in the box. It's filled with her grandmother's jewelry. She's opened it a hundred times, tried on every ring and bracelet. But every time her grandmother hands her the box, she feels a rush of anticipation, as if she's opening it for the first time.

Stephanie thinks of this when her grandmother comes to the store. Corinne will not leave until she's examined each one of Stephanie's hundred or so pieces. She runs her fingers along each lovingly finished edge, recognizing the cool of the metal, the curve of a stone, the strength and invention that has passed down through the generations to her granddaughter's soul.

The pain was there in the morning, like a premonition.
Margaret Mildred Gray ignored it.

It was the day of the annual Tribal Dances, a June gathering that the Osage Nation looked forward to all year.

Of the many locals who would be celebrated, Margaret had a position of special significance. She was one of the most revered of the tribe's elders, a woman who in her youth had been honored as a tribal princess, had songs written for her and pictures painted of her, and had married Buddy Gray, a man who would become an Osage drumkeeper, a ceremonial leader, and a legend.

She and her husband had raised their seven children according to the Osage ways and according to their Catholic faith. Most of all, the children learned early on that they were born to a great responsibility—to right a wrong, to make a difference.

The results were evident. Each of the Gray children would gain prominence in very different fields: Gina with her artwork; Andrew as a roadman, or leader, of the Native American church; Margo with an engineering firm and as a business leader recognized throughout the nation; Jacque as a spiritual leader; Louis as a civil rights activist and national leader in the fight to ban Indian-named mascots; Mary as one of best ribbon workers in the tribe. The youngest child, Jim Gray, became chief of the Osage Nation and is widely regarded as future candidate for national office.

So on this June day, with the heat bearing down on the reservation land, there was much to celebrate. Margaret did not want to acknowledge the pain gaining strength in her body or the chill that she couldn't seem to shake off.

Margaret Gray

Margaret Gray outside her family home in Pawhuska, Oklahoma.

When a grandmother has a heart attack at a family gathering, the hospital waiting room can become a crowded place. When that grandmother has seven children, twenty-seven grandchildren, and twenty-seven great-grandchildren, the waiting room becomes a city of its own.

When word of Margaret's illness reached the camp where the dances were to take place, the celebration turned into a mass procession down the winding, sloping road that runs from Pawhuska to the hospital in Bartlesville.

By nightfall, doctors assured Margaret's children that she would recover, that they'd caught the blockage in her heart in time. But by then, her family had shut down the festivities.

Six months later, on Margaret's eightieth birthday, the family has gathered again, this time at Margaret's home in one of the new ranch houses that the tribe has built for their elders atop a hill. On the road in front of Margaret's home, cars arrive at parade pace. Each new arrival rushes first to Margaret for a hug and birthday wishes. She's uncomfortable with all the attention, but oh, how she loves each member of her family, down to the smallest great-grandchild, who runs up to her, screaming, "Mimi!"

"My husband and I were both orphans, and we just always wanted a big family. We were named Indian Family of the Year in 2003, and people always say, 'How did you do it?' Well, you know, I'm just very, very blessed. I didn't do anything. It's my children that have made so much progress."

Out on the porch, Margaret's children offer a very different perspective. They describe a mother and grandmother who, along with their charismatic father, created a world apart, a place where they felt chal-lenged and protected, where they never saw alcohol or heard a swear word or knew that there were men who did not hold their wives in the highest regard.

"So many Indian families are just taught to cower down in the corner, and that never was us," Margo says. "We come from this rich background in our culture and in our family," says Louis. "Dad and Mom said all the time, 'To whom much is given, much is expected.'"

Both their father and mother drummed into them a sense of respon-sibility, not just to their family and to the Osage Nation, but to the extended world they'd come to know. Why just own and run a business if you could help others build their own businesses? Why just support the Osage Nation when you could represent it and fight for change?

"We relied a lot on ourselves and each other," Gina recalls. "We really bonded. You have this team, an automatic team for cleaning and playing, but Mom really had a way of helping every one of us find what our strength was and rise to the top.

"I think we've all tried to replicate that and to give our kids that by allowing them to build their own relationships with Mom."

As her children began to have children of their own, Margaret recalls running to the hospital seem-ingly once a week to see a new grandchild. She became the de facto mother, and it was understood that she would step in to raise any of the grandchildren at times when the parents were called away for work or needed to return to school.

Margaret's sons and daughters tried to recreate with their children the childhood they knew. But their families were no longer insulated from the outside world, and their children have had to steel themselves against forces that would draw them away from their grandmother's values. For that generation, Margaret is viewed as not just influential, but critical to their survival.

"Mom is the stabilizing force in our family, especially for the younger kids," Andrew says.

"It's not that we weren't touched by alcohol and divorce; we were," Jacque says of her sisters and brothers and their children. "But it didn't come from Mom and Dad. It was getting out in that crazy world and finding it crazy. If you're asking me where our children would be if it weren't for Mom, I can tell you, and I feel certain about this: Some of them would be dead right now."

"She's the glue that holds this family together," Jim says. "We all go out and find our way. But we always come back and are comforted by Mom's ability to comfort us emotionally. We know how much she wants us to do the right thing, and we don't want to disappoint."

They all worry about losing her, and what that would mean not just for them as a family, but for the Osage Nation, which relies on its elders as keepers of the tribe's culture and wisdom. "You can't imagine the depth of loss when you contemplate it," Andrew says. "Everything is passed down orally; it's not written down. Not just with the Osage, but across the whole tribal community."

As Margaret joins them on the porch, she urges them away from stories about her. She wants to talk about their achievements, particularly her son Jim's election as chief.

She remembers standing with crowds of family members across the street from town headquarters where votes were being tallied. It seemed like hours went by, and every so often, one kid or another would run across the street to get an update. There was a count, a recount. Jim began to worry about losing a close election and was on the phone with his attorney, reviewing his options.

Then, finally, Louis ran out the door and across the street shouting, "You won, you won!"

"It was like a dream come true," Margaret recalls.

"Louis laughs at the memory of the group of them, jumping atop each other, yelling out their victory. "I'd like to say we were real classy, but we all squealed."

"We did," Margaret laughs. "We screamed like banshees. I was the worst. I couldn't believe it." She remembers standing amid her children, wondering for the millionth time at the grace that brought her to that moment. With the June sky stretched above her, she gazed at the circles of offspring around her and declared with enormous pride, "I'm now the mother of the chief."

At twenty-two, Rita Chopra was beginning a new life in the United States.

She and her new husband, Deepak, had just moved from India to New Jersey and then Boston where he had come to continue his medical training. Rita and Deepak left behind their extended family in Dehli and all that was familiar

They were both well educated children of traditional families. Rita had gone to college, but set aside further education so that her husband could pursue his career. This seemed right to her. In India, both she and Deepak had been raised in homes where becoming a mother was one of life's greatest honors, and where the grandmother was the center of family life. Rita looked forward to taking on the important cultural role of mother, and planned to have a baby. But at gatherings with new friends and colleagues, she soon discovered that in America, the role of mother did not hold such honor. "But what do you *do*?" Rita was asked over and over, as if her ambitions of becoming pregnant and having a family were hardly enough.

"I used to feel, what *am* I doing?" Rita says. Rita had always been confident, quietly secure. But all around her, educated women were embracing feminist ideals that challenged the very traditions so central to Indian life. "We were surrounded by very accomplished people, and there was a great deal of pressure."

Alone in a foreign country, with two young children and a husband who worked around the clock, Rita looked inside herself and found that she was realizing the very ambition she feared she'd lost. As a mother and now a grandmother, she is core of a large, extended family, the person whom everyone turns to first for advice, for help, for comfort. First in Boston and then in San Diego and La Jolla, Rita's created a home that is open, a place that is the center

Rita Chopra, Leela & Tara Mandal

Leela Mandal, Rita Chopra, and Tara Mandal in Rita's Manhattan apartment.

of activity for cousins and neighbors and friends.

While her husband, Deepak Chopra became known around the world for his ability to repair injuries to individuals, communities, and nations, Rita has become the mender and sustainer of her family's soul.

"She's the one who makes sure that everyone's taken care of, whether it's emotionally, financially, socially," says her daughter Mallika Chopra, the mother of her two grandchildren, who has just published a book about motherhood. "She is the absolute foundation for all of our lives, the touchstone and treasure trove of love and compassion."

The Chopra name is synonymous with new-age philosophies of spiritual and physical health. Deepak Chopra draws on ancient teachings and modern medicine to promote a philosophy of wellness of body and mind that has become increasingly popular. He has sold more than twenty million copies of some forty books. His Chopra Center for Well Being in La Jolla, California, draws devotees from around the world. Among his fans are the Dalai Lama and Nobel Laureate Desmond Tutu. He is a regular on talk shows and the lecture circuit. Rita, in turn, is now the revered grandmother figure so important in Indian culture.

"I had amazing role models," she says. "*Readers Digest* used to have this item about the most unforgettable person you know, and that's who my own grandmother was: a real matriarch who ran the whole family." Though she was uneducated and married by the age of fourteen, she taught Rita the power one person has to be an organizing force in a family and help shape the lives of those around her. "She had fourteen grandchildren, and was involved in every decision in every one of their lives." She knew Rita should marry him even before Rita did. "She was the real matriarch," says Rita.

A few days after Christmas, the Chopra family gathers in a New York apartment just before Deepak and Rita are to leave for India, where Deepak is to promote is new book, *Peace is the Way*. Rita is just as happy to pursue her own adventures and passion for history and Indian art, Deepak by all accounts relies on her in the way the rest of the family does, for spiritual sustenance.

On this day, he has run to the toy store to buy yet another trinket for his granddaughters; daughter Mallika had a meeting with the publisher of her forthcoming book. Though her husband, Sumant, is around, Mallika knew without asking that her mother would take care of Tara, who is nearly three, and baby Leela, six months old. Only when Rita mentioned that she was to have her picture taken and that perhaps she should take time to do something with her hair did Mallika realize that once again, her mother had put her own needs last; in the end, Rita told Mallika not to worry, that in the scheme of things, the way her hair looked hardly mattered.

She relaxes into an armchair with Leela on her lap, Tara running from her grandmother to her father and back. From where Rita sits, she can look through the apartment's sizeable windows to the winter streets of Midtown Manhattan.

"If Mallika needs to travel, or the grandchildren need something, I'm going to be there. Personally, I am quite happy being a homemaker. When we were first starting out, that was hard for me to accept. But I see

ence was transformative. "It is such a wonderful tradition."

At the time, Mallika was finishing her MBA at Northwestern University, where her husband, Sumant, had graduated two years earlier. Rita commuted from her San Diego home to Evanston, Illinois, throughout the pregnancy so that Mallika could stay on track with her schooling.

"I felt that it was important that Mallika have every opportunity," Rita says. "I finished college, but I never went beyond that. I made the right choice for me. But Mallika has to make that choice for herself, and I wanted her to have all the resources she needed so she could do that."

When the baby came, Rita and Deepak were at the hospital and able to hold their first grandchild only twenty minutes after she was born. "It was amazing," Rita says. "People tell you, but you can't imagine the feeling."

For the next forty days, Rita cooked meals, washed clothes, and tended to the errands that a new mother can't do. In those early days, and in the years since, Rita has often been struck by the great wisdom that inspired this arrangement.

"I have literally been with these children from the day they were born," she says. "It is a kind of love that one has never experienced, or that I don't remember from when Mallika was born. I think at the age I was then, you just take it for granted."

now that if I hadn't been there to fill in the gaps, with all that Deepak was doing, we wouldn't have a life.' "

When Tara was born, Mallika moved into her mother's home for forty days, as is Indian tradition. She slept in her mother's bed, and Rita cared for the baby and the new mother. "My baby would wake up and I would feed her and then Mom would take her for the night," Mallika recalls. "She was, once again, the epitome of motherhood." For Rita, the experi-

Now, Rita cannot go a week without seeing the girls. She imagines a time when she can travel with both girls, show them the world. But for now, she must leave the grandchildren behind. She's trying to prepare herself. "I was supposed to be in India for six weeks, but I've already cut it to four weeks." She sighs and considers whether she can cut the trip even further. "How long can I be away from them? We'll just have to see."

In the fall of 1981, just before she was to leave her refugee camp
for the United States, Kimeng Ven ventured back to her village

*Kimeng Ven
& Jessica Nem*

*Jessica Nem and Kimeng Ven
in Chicago, Illinois.*

in Cambodia in search of some remnant of the home where she'd raised her children or the life she'd once known.

She was fifty years old, skeletal from four years of forced labor. The Khmer Rouge had turned her already war-torn country into a mass grave. She had lost her husband, four of her five children, and her home. Her life seemed always to hang on the edge of extinction. To survive, she buried her feelings and thoughts; she tried to be just another black-clad, laboring body, barely distinguishable from those around her.

She'd escaped to Thailand with her one surviving son and a beloved niece. There she'd received a chance to go the United States.

Kimeng did not know the language or the country's customs, and she barely knew the cousin who was sponsoring them. Who would she be there? She was still a mother, but now a grandmother, too; her son had married and become a father while in the refugee camp. The infant was named Jessica— an American name.

She'd returned to her village with the hope of finding something to take to America with her. But as her land and then her home came into view, she saw that it was now a military site, used first by the Khmer Rouge and now the

Vietnamese occupiers. She searched the area where, in the hours before they fled the village, she'd buried silver and photographs and whatever else she could find of value. But those were gone, too.

It was as if her life had evaporated. She could not imagine what would replace it.

More than two decades later, Kimeng remains a woman who is skilled in the art of invisibility. She is no longer bony and angular, but rounded, of average height, with eyeglasses that make her eyes appear larger and farther apart than they actually are. Though she once took English classes, she rarely uses the language and speaks with hesitancy.

Kimeng's granddaughter, Jessica Nem, serves as translator and an empowering voice. Jessica, at twenty-four, has striking eyes and the slowly expressive face of someone accustomed to talking with the very old and very young. She juggles a job, a first mortgage, a new boyfriend, and preparations for an MBA; an equation that is as foreign to Kimeng as the authority with which Jessica speaks of them.

But in the kitchen, it is Kimeng who is in command, cooking elaborate dishes, telling stories, creating a stew of aromas and images that transport Jessica to a place she's never been. Every day, Kimeng cares for Jessica's youngest brother, who is ten, and cooks meals for members of their extended family. She's known for her ability to cater to diverse appetites, adding shrimp for Jessica's father, eliminating vegetables for her little brother.

When Jessica was little, she recalls,
she and her grandmother had a way of talking,
of being together,
that felt different from her relationship with everyone else.

For Jessica, cooking alongside her grandmother is akin to traveling with her to a place where the future and past collide, a metaphor for the indirect way her grandmother has helped define the person Jessica has become.

"She would never tell me this is right or wrong, or you should be generous and think of others," Jessica says. "And I think there are parts of my life that she doesn't exactly understand. But if you look at her while she's cooking, she's always telling stories, and the stories almost always have a moral."

"My parents always worked, and she was always there with me, so really, she probably did more in terms of influencing me than even my parents," Jessica continues. Kimeng raised not only Jessica and her two brothers, but helped raise her five cousins as well, walking them to school, waiting for them to come home in the afternoons. "She takes care of my friends, too. So many of my friends who are Cambodian don't have grandmothers, so she's always been kind of the community grandma. She's the only grandmother they'll ever have."

Even when Jessica was little, she recalls, she and her grandmother had a way of talking, of being together, that felt different from her relationship with everyone else. While the young Jessica might not share particulars of a given relationship or her anxieties about a test in school,

her grandmother could sense the girl's emotion. In response, Kimeng would tell her a story, a parable that almost always highlighted animals and most certainly offered up a lesson about enduring what you can't abide or finding good in the midst of evil.

So powerful were the stories that Jessica insisted to a first-grade teacher that, in Cambodia, animals talked in just the way her grandmother had taught her. The teacher could not persuade her otherwise.

"My friends always kid me, saying that I talk in metaphors. That's just one small way my grandmother has influenced me," Jessica says. "It's not like I go to her for advice with boyfriends, but she is definitely the one who taught me what's right and wrong."

As Jessica grew older, her grandmother's importance in her life only increased, especially in 1996, when her parents told her they were getting divorced. Though divorce is common in America, it is far less acceptable among the community of traditional Cambodian families and relatives among whom Jessica was raised. They were families of new immigrants who relied on each other for guidance and support.

Jessica felt isolated from her immediate family and from her extended one. She acted out, both as an American teenager and as a daughter of Cambodian parents who themselves were defying tradition.

"I was fifteen and very rebellious," Jessica recalls. "The divorce caused such a big rift. My family was falling apart, and we didn't have immediate support."

Jessica's mother moved out, and her youngest brother, a toddler, was too young to understand what was happening. Jessica bore the weight of her family's dismay. "There was a feeling that I'd gone astray," she says. "I wasn't doing well in high school, and education had always been so important."

Only her grandmother could reach her. Kimeng did not offer judgments; she listened and she told stories, and through those stories, Jessica began to piece together her grandmother's past and all she had endured.

At the same time, she felt free to express her own anger and frustration and never felt as though her anguish was somehow diminished by her grandmother's more painful past.

But there are moments when her grandmother will describe an experience or detail, a death so jarring that Jessica has a hard time reconciling the woman who soothes her pain and cooks so passionately with the one who has witnesses a mother kill a child.

Whether talking to a stranger or to family, Kimeng describes her final years in Cambodia through the dispassion of recollected facts—the number of days they walked from her home through the killing fields to the jungle where they built a hut—but rarely does she speak of the emotional toll.

Instead, she urges Jessica to share the ways in which Kimeng sees herself and her daughters in Jessica. "We're both monkeys in the zodiac, for instance," Jessica says, both of them laughing. In the kitchen, they share a hunger for fine food, for Kimeng's stories, for a past that Jessica knows is in the person she has become. She recalls with delight a day just recently when her grandmother asked her for a recipe—a nod that Jessica took as the highest form of praise. Her grandmother's accomplishments, the eight grandchildren she's helped raise, the endless cooking of meals and satisfying of so many appetites, the wiping of tears, is not the visible kind of work that Jessica knows gets rewards and notice.

Jessica felt her grandmother's pride when, at age twenty, she graduated college with two degrees and high honors. She knows that her grandmother wants her to pursue her advanced degree in business, and she's working toward that. She's arrived at this point, she knows, in part because of her grandmother's resilience and the lessons that have come from that.

"I know," Jessica says, tears gathering in her eyes, "I know she's proud of me."

Her grandmother leans forward and with her palm wipes the tears from her granddaughter's cheek.

Some years ago, Frances Sternhagen
counted among her favorite characters

one she called "the haughty lady." Performing the haughty lady made her one of the leading character actresses of her generation, honored by two Tony Awards and four nominations for her roles in Broadway shows. She's the matriarch on television shows such as *ER*, where she played Dr. Carter's overbearing grandmother, or on *Cheers* and *Sex and the City*. She's been playing the haughty lady a long time—so long that, early on, the role required an ingenious leap of acting imagination; her first performance was at the age of seven.

"I was an only child, and that means that you spend a lot of time with adults. My parents had some pretty interesting and eccentric friends who were fun to imitate," she says. Frances also had a next-door neighbor— her best friend—who was blessed with a wealthy, imperious grandmother of her own.

"We made the ladies outrageous. They were very snobbish and very snooty and they would make absolute fools of themselves. We would call our chauffeurs (James and Johnson) and pretend to be driven in these very fancy limousine cars to odd places, like restaurants where we would go into the kitchen and complain about the food."

It is a measure of Frances's acting prowess that she is so convincing as the pompous grandmother who wouldn't be caught dead without her

Frances
Sternhagen,
Julia & Payton
Carlin

Frances Sternhagen, Julia Carlin, and Payton Carlin in Frances's backyard in New Rochelle, New York.

pearls. Because in real life, Frances is decidedly unassuming in a vintage skirt and sensible walking shoes, her gray mane of hair pulled haphazardly into a barrette. She has six children and six grandchildren, but in her seventies she pursues her work with as much passion and determination as she did in her forties. "I'm not what you would call an ideal grandmother in the way you'd think of someone who is always around and does all sorts of fun things," she says.

But the center of Frances's relationship with all her grandkids is the family house. It is a rambling, three-story structure on a leafy street in New Rochelle, forty minutes away from New York City. Frances and her late husband, the actor Thomas Carlin, moved there in 1959. At a time when families are transient and grandmothers are often far away, Frances has created a home that has a powerful identity and a reach that extends far beyond New Rochelle into her children's and grandchildren's lives.

"The house is this magical, mysterious place," says grandson Justin Morse, who is studying writing and land sciences in Columbus, Ohio. "It's kind of like a family member, the big nonliving one who holds everyone together, and Frannie created it; she seems to be the electricity that runs through it."

For Frances, running the house is a labor of love; it's a place she returns to in lieu of taking an apartment in the city during a rigorous performing schedule on Broadway. Inside the house, barely a surface is not covered: Framed pictures appear to have been there for decades alongside snapshots that might have been developed last week. There are piles of magazines and books, shells of horseshoe crabs and dried sand dollars, and pieces of driftwood that speak of a lifetime of adventure.

Frances is at the kitchen table, where the Sunday edition of the *New York Times* is spread on the table, the sunlight forming geometric patterns on the floor. Granddaughter Julia is outside in the yard playing with cousin Payton. "You know, there has been such a shift in families," Frances says. "People are so much more mobile. It's no longer the way it was in the fifties or even the thirties, when people wanted something that provides continuity and stability for the kids."

When she and Thomas moved into the house in 1959, the neighborhood was filled with large families and creative types, writers and actors who commuted to Manhattan and often worked from home. It was never assumed that Frances would stay home, and Thomas proved to be more comfortable in the role of the parent who invents games and teaches the kids to play ball. His acting career eventually faltered, while Frances was working around the clock. But she turned down jobs that required extensive travel and helped create an atmosphere in the neighborhood and in the house that inspired a type of nostalgic fun that is hard to find today.

Amanda Carlin, Frances's daughter, who is an actress in Los Angeles, and Payton's father, Paul Carlin, a New York–based director and actor, describe a childhood that extended down the street to a boathouse where there were sailboats, canoes, surfboards, and access to Long Island Sound. The Carlin kids all had extensive chores but also played hard, traveling from backyard to backyard and to the boathouse with abandon.

But work defined their mother. "She was not maternal as a mother, and she's not maternal as a grandmother," Amanda says. "But she also is this example of someone who is prolific and working, which is its own gift."

bers Frannie stringing lights through the big old trees that line the street outside her home and organizing a square dance with live music and a makeshift stage. Equally memorable are the annual Christmas Eve parties.

"My grandma creates these amazing little books with drawings on the cover that someone in the family has done, and inside the books are Christmas carols," Justin says. "At some point, we all gather around the piano and sing, and it's this wonderful feeling you don't want to miss."

For the younger grandchildren, like Julia or Payton, the house is as perfect a setting for hide-and-seek as a kid is likely to find. There are three floors and endless hiding places—a cupboard under the stairs, a nook under the drawers in the kitchen—and an attic playroom, complete with a ladder along the ceiling and a huge, old dollhouse that Frances picked up at a church rummage sale when her children were little.

But the kids don't relate to their grandmother the way an adult grandchild such as Justin does. He remembers seeing his grandmother perform *The Heiress*. As she walked onto the stage, the audience burst into spontaneous applause before she even uttered a word, and the moment made his hair stand on end. He was eleven when he first heard her perform a monologue. It was a private performance at his dining-room table, and he remembers seeing his father moved to tears.

"There's some point like a threshold that you cross when you see her as this pretty incredible woman, when you relate to her more as an adult," he says.

"She used to joke that she had six of us so that we could take care of one another, because she was afraid she wouldn't know what to do with just one," Amanda says.

Justin, her first grandchild, called her "Frannie," a name that his mother, Sarah, and Frances settled on after Frances rejected "Grandma" with a wrinkle of her nose. Now that he is twenty-three, Justin has a rich relationship with his grandmother: They'll talk for hours in her kitchen, trading ideas and stories while she's finishing the dishes.

As a young child, her grandson lived at the house for a time. He remem-

Even when she was a young actress, Frances found that directors cast her in roles of complex, usually older women. She was Daisy in the stage version of *Driving Miss Daisy*, Aunt Lavinia in *The Heiress*, Ida in *Mornings at Seven*. She is an actress as anthropologist, digging deep for the quirky details that define people. Over time, she has chosen roles by the depth of the character rather than the size of the part.

"I was really lucky because the work was always there," she says.

That is not always the case, especially in the film industry, where at forty-six women can find it hard to find challenging roles. "In Europe and England, there is so much more respect for, number one, age, and, number two, eccentricity. Some of the grandmothers in the scripts I've been asked to look at for television have been absolutely insulting to older women and I've thought, *I don't want to take that. It's a rehash of clichés, it's been done before*."

At the moment, Frances is performing in the stage version of *Steel Magnolias* on Broadway. For the youngest of her grandchildren, the acting is mostly a distraction, something that takes their grandmother away from them.

"Why are you always working?" Julia asks her grandmother. They are

in the backyard, Julia and cousin Payton running among the trees and wooden swing set. The two kids are a few weeks apart in age, but Julia seems more attached to Frances, following her from kitchen to backyard, urging her to sit on the swings.

Frances is about to answer when Julia decides instead to lead a tour up to the third-floor playroom. Perhaps Julia senses that her grandmother's work is important to her in a way she doesn't yet understand. Or perhaps she knows that by running to the playroom, where her mother and aunts and uncles played and where her grandmother built furniture for a dollhouse, she is as close to Frannie as she would be if she were on her lap.

"Maybe as a kid you don't get this at first, but I think you sense it," Justin says. "The house is her. It has this great warmth; it is about family in the truest sense, this place where you can go year after year, and you know everything around you might be changing, but this place changes slowly so that it's there, with the garden in back, and there's music and movies and playing cards after dinner. It's reliable, always there, a great, great feeling."